Surge and Thunder

Surge and Thunder

Critical Readings in Homer's Odyssey

D. M. GAUNT

SENIOR LECTURER IN CLASSICS, UNIVERSITY OF BRISTOL

Men hear, like Ocean on a Western beach,
The surge and thunder of the Odyssey.
                                        Andrew Lang

OXFORD UNIVERSITY PRESS 1971

Oxford University Press   *Ely House, London W.1*

Glasgow	Bombay
New York	Calcutta
Toronto	Madras
Melbourne	Karachi
Wellington	Lahore
Cape Town	Dacca
Salisbury	Kuala Lumpur
Ibadan	Singapore
Nairobi	Hong Kong
Dar es Salaam	Tokyo
Lusaka	
Addis Ababa	

Photoset by BAS Printers Limited, Wallop, Hampshire.
Printed in Great Britain by
Redwood Press Ltd., Trowbridge, Wiltshire.

Dedicated to the people of Dent
in the West Riding of Yorkshire,
where this book was conceived
and first took shape.

τρηχεῖ᾽, ἀλλ᾽ ἀγαθὴ κουροτρόφος

A rough land, but a good nurse of real men
                                        Od. ix. 27

Preface

A reviewer in the *Times Literary Supplement* said not long ago*
'It is the whole fabric of writing which creates the effect on
the audience intended by the author, and it is in making
intelligible these language-bound elements that the classical
scholar can best help those who are confined by their own
language.' This book is an attempt to give such help. It is
intended not for professional scholars but for the many readers
of Homer's *Odyssey* who have no Greek and must therefore be
content with a second-hand version of his poem. Something of
its quality may be conveyed even by a prose version, but the
power and colour of the original will always be much weakened.
My aim has been to translate a number of interesting passages
of varying length in such a way as to give an accurate but read-
able version, and then, in the appreciations, one of which is
attached to each passage, to explain some points of language
and fine shades of meaning which no translation can hope to
convey. These appreciations seek only to help readers towards
that state of mind which Gilbert Murray once described** as
'living again in understanding and imagination the great hours
that have once been lived'; that is, feeling for oneself the reactions which any competent Greek scholar might be expected
to have, provided that he were handling the text as literature
and not as a quarry for material relevant to the study of grammar, syntax, history, archaeology, textual criticism or any of
the other topics which so often seem to interest classical
scholars more than the poetry itself. Some of the criticism
springs from a study of the language, some of it is interpreta-
tive in a more general way. Where the passages are lengthy,
additional material not immediately connected with the

* 4 January, 1968, in a review of H. D. F. Kitto's *Poiesis* (California, 1966).
** *An Unfinished Autobiography*, p.145 (London, 1960).

appreciation has sometimes been supplied in the form of a commentary.

Homer's style has a texture and quality of its own, and this question I treat separately in the Introduction, which is intended to help the reader to approach the individual passages in the right frame of mind. It is not there possible to proceed immediately to stylistic matters; only after a brief consideration of the nature of oral epic in general can one go on to a study of Homer's own style as a background to the selected passages which form the core of the book.

It is necessary to add a word about the translations themselves. T. R. Glover held that a translation 'should reproduce on the mind of the new reader, in the new language, as far as may be, the emotional, intellectual and spiritual effect (perhaps reaction would be the more precise word) that the original produced, and was intended to produce, on the readers in the original speech'.* But this asks too much. We cannot know precisely what effect the *Odyssey* produced, or was intended to produce, on its original hearers, though we may be able to make some reasoned guesses such as are contained in the Introduction; and because our circumstances are so different, we can hardly hope actually to share their reactions. The translations in this book have the simpler aim of transmitting the effect which the passages have on the translator, so that by this means the reader may have access, as far as this is possible, to the poem itself; in the end every student of Homer wishes, in Dame Helen Gardner's phrase, to be 'left alone with the poem'.**

* Tertullian, Loeb ed., Intro.
** Helen Gardner, *The Business of Criticism,* p.17 (Oxford, 1959).

Contents

Introduction

Homer as Poet and Story-teller

.1. The twentieth-century reader who picks up a modern version of the *Odyssey* will probably enjoy it, however little he knows about epic poetry or the Greek language; for the poem contains so many good things that, even when it has been mangled by translation and stripped of all its original beauty of language, it retains some of its compelling power. However, under these conditions the reader is receiving a 'signal' so much weakened by all this interference that he cannot really be said to be 'reading Homer' at all. The poem was composed nearly 3,000 years ago in a world so unlike our own that the only immediate point of contact for the Greekless reader lies in the unchanging nature of human emotions; consequently a real effort of the imagination is necessary if we are to make the most of the text in our hands. One of the results of the growing importance given to scientific studies is that men are beginning to forget the true nature of literature. Great writers do not merely pass on facts which can be coded, digested and regurgitated by a computer; they are, whether they know it or not, telling us about their world and their situation, and in order to do so they must use the words of their mother-tongue. Greek was a language of great subtlety even in those early days when the *Odyssey* was composed. Homeric words and phrases carry overtones and subtleties of meaning which it is still possible for us to understand in some measure; the extant material is on a large scale, so that we have a good deal of evidence to work on. It is the business of the appreciations and commentaries to deal with such points. But in addition the reader will require some knowledge of the fundamental nature of Homeric poetry, concerning which it has been well said that it was 'a real and living language; it was to the vernacular

Note Matters discussed in the Introduction may be related to what follows by the use of the Index of Literary Topics.

what dancing is to walking – a stylized behaviour perfected for the purpose of fine art. It was no doubt the creation of many centuries and had been used and heard and understood times out of mind'.* The flavour of this ancient style is not easily recaptured, but the following pages are intended to give some idea of its nature.

2. The text of the *Odyssey* may have been written down for the first time in the eighth century B.C., but the poem had a long history before that moment. The fall of the great mainland power of Mycenae probably occurred in the twelfth century B.C., and it seems likely that bards were singing to noble audiences long before that date. We see a picture of such a performance at *Od. viii.* 256 ff., where the blind bard Demodocus sings to amuse and entertain the Phaeacian nobility. Whenever a bard sings in this way he is retelling an old story, but he is also in a real sense recreating it. He is the intermediary between the tale and the hearers, whose enjoyment will depend not only on his memory and technique, but also on his involvement. The scene must exist in his imagination while he describes it, and the techniques which he uses are devices which enable him to liberate his imagination for the purposes of this re-creation. Some of these techniques are very relevant to the passages to be examined in this book, and it will be worth while to spend time considering them. In view of the emphasis which we shall lay on these oral techniques, it is, however, necessary to add that the poems as we have them do not appear to be wholly oral; it seems possible that Homer himself (or his amanuensis) had a knowledge of writing, and was therefore able to conduct some sort of revision of what he had composed. This would, of course, be impossible for a fully oral poet, for whom a poem exists only as and when he utters it. The structure of the *Iliad* and *Odyssey* is so complex that many scholars find it difficult to believe that they were composed by wholly oral methods.

* H. T. Wade-Gery, *The Poet of the Iliad*, p. 39 (Cambridge, 1952).

3. The nature of oral poetry is by no means simple. Fortunately it is still practised in some parts of the world, and the invention of the tape-recorder has enabled scholars to study it closely.* The singer, who has a memory so accurate that among book-readers it would pass for prodigious, grows up in a society where many tales are in circulation. Usually trained by an older bard, he will have a large repertoire of stories, to which he can make impromptu additions with amazing versatility. He does not, however, reproduce his tales verbatim. There appear, in fact, to be several separate aids to memory, whose combined use will produce a story capable of expansion, contraction and other alterations designed to suit a particular audience or a particular occasion. First, there is the plot of the story itself, which is firm in the singer's mind, but only in outline; some episodes, such as the story of Dolon in *Iliad x.*, will be 'optional'. Secondly, there are the characters. No doubt the characters of the major heroes were all firmly 'set' in the tradition; they were obligatory, and the bard's only freedom was to contract or elaborate. This, as we shall see, is a very important freedom. Second-rank heroes, about whom the bard would inherit a much smaller body of information, offer more scope for invention; it seems that Telemachus, for example, may well have been Homer's own creation. Minor characters are often 'from stock', although occasionally one meets originality – Elpenor, for example, who was 'not very bright' (*Od. x.* 553), and fell off a flat roof. Thirdly, there are certain 'themes' which recur constantly in heroic verse – such occasions as arming oneself for battle, making a sacrifice or setting sail. (Cf. Passage I) These form 'stock passages', which are frequently repeated verbatim. It has been well observed** that a succession of such themes may form 'a thematic structure' which will give particular effects such as 'escalation', 'foreshadowing' or 'posturing'. The audience would no doubt

---

* See especially: A. B. Lord, *Singer of Tales;* C. M. Bowra, *Heroic Poetry* (cf. Bibliography).
** Cf. T. M. Andersson, *The Icelandic Family Saga*, ch. 2 (Harvard, 1967).

feel a subconscious expectation that the story, as it developed, would yield, in the hands of a skilled singer, such well-known effects. Thus when, in *Odyssey ix*, Odysseus taunts the Cyclops, thereby provoking a response which nearly results in his own death and that of his companions, his 'showing off' represents a pattern of behaviour common to most Homeric heroes; and when, at the Phaeacian games, Odysseus is challenged by Euryalus, this is the beginning of an 'escalation-pattern' which might easily have led through a predictable series of events to an ugly incident. In such cases we are dealing with a pattern of behaviour which, just because it is predictable, is no less helpful to the singer than the 'stock passages' mentioned above. The stock passages themselves would gradually settle into a fixed form of words, so that for any one bard they would be constant; and they are very common in both the *Odyssey* and the *Iliad*. Finally, the poet has at his command a wide range of phrases which fit certain particular places in the line. These are the 'formulae',* for the understanding of which further explanation is necessary.

4. Homer's poetry, like virtually all poetry written in Greek and Latin, was composed in a 'quantitative' metre. The concept is unfamiliar to most modern readers, yet it is impossible to obtain any idea of the 'feel' of the poem unless it is understood.

5. English verse is scanned by word-stresses; that is, we stress certain syllables in each word by forcing more air than usual over the vocal chords when we come to the syllable in question. It is only by attending to these stresses that we can form any idea of the metre of a poem. Thus, when we read Milton's line

In ádamántine chaíns and pénal fíre

we recognize the pattern of an unstressed followed by a stressed syllable, five times repeated, which we call blank verse. There are complications over counter-stressing, when

* See also Passage XIII, Appreciation, 2-4.

in a particular foot the stresses are reversed,* but the principle is clear.

6. Greek words also had stresses,** but these are of no importance in determining scansion. The important thing in a quantitative metre is the length of time which a syllable takes to utter. By convention, a syllable must be either 'long' or 'short', and one long syllable is equivalent to two shorts. A syllable is considered to be long if it contains a vowel long by nature or, supposing the vowel to be short, if it contains two consonants following the vowel. Again there are exceptions, but this is the underlying principle. The Homeric hexameter is a 'dactylic' line of six 'feet'; that is, its basic unit is one long syllable followed by two shorts (a dactyl), and this is six times repeated; but in the first four feet of the line a 'spondee' (two longs) may be substituted for the dactyl, and the sixth foot never contains more than two syllables. The pattern may be represented as follows:

If we apply this pattern to an actual line, we obtain the following results

$$\overset{1}{n\acute{u}mphe}\,\overset{2}{p\acute{o}tn\breve{\i}}\,'\,\overset{3}{\breve{e}r\acute{u}k\breve{e}}\,\overset{4}{K\bar{a}l\acute{u}ps\bar{o}},\,\overset{5}{d\breve{\i}\breve{a}}\,\overset{6}{th\acute{e}\bar{a}\bar{o}n}\,{***}$$

('The nymph of power detained him, Calypso, divine among goddesses'), where we see a spondee $(-\,-)$ in the first, fourth and sixth feet, and a dactyl $(-\cup\cup)$ in the second, third and fifth (where it is obligatory). The word-stresses may or may not correspond with the initial long syllable of each foot. In the line above they do so, as is shown by the diacritical marks,

---

* e.g. Broúght déath ínto the world and all our woe, where the first foot contains two stresses and the second is counter-stressed.
** They had a pitch-accent too, like Welsh.
*** Cf. Guide to Pronunciation.

each of which is placed over a stressed syllable. In the following line, however, they fall differently:

tén d'ắpắmēibŏmĕnōs prŏsĕphē nĕphĕlĕgĕrĕtă Zéus
('And to her in answer spoke cloud-gatherer Zeus.')

Here in each foot there is a stress which does not fall on the first syllable. In neither case have the stresses any effect in determining the scansion, though the 'conflict' between the movement of the metre and the placing of the word-stresses is always perceptible to the listening ear and is one of the charms of quantitative verse; it is the quantities which determine the metre. Consequently the length of each vowel sound is of the greatest importance for scansion, and it is noteworthy that in Greek two of the five vowels (e and o) have different alphabetical symbols according to whether they are to be pronounced short or long. In almost all cases correct pronunciation is essential if the metre is to be preserved. In this book, whenever lines of Greek are transliterated, both quantities and stresses are indicated so that the reader can arrive at an approximate pronunciation.

7. Although there are plenty of 'over-run' or 'enjambed' lines in Homer, the majority end with some kind of pause, and it seems that the line was the basic unit of composition, as indeed one would expect. A 'theme' could be expanded or contracted by the insertion or omission of non-essential lines, and there are many instances of this. For example, the passages in the *Iliad* where a hero arms himself for battle vary greatly in length, and it seems that the poet made them longer or shorter to fit his view of the importance of the situation. When a poem was being sung, the nature and reactions of the audience would also be a factor.

8. In the Homeric poems there are several places where a bard or a hero is described as singing to the accompaniment of the lyre, as his modern Jugoslav counterpart does with his one-stringed 'gusle'. It seems likely that the lyre was not so much a musical accompaniment as a means of emphas-

izing the movement of the metre, which must have been
strongly perceived by both bard and audience. It may also have
helped concentration, and Professor E. A. Havelock has
recently suggested* that the 'personal commitment' of all
those present at a recital must have been almost total. It is
certain that we, who are accustomed to take in our literary
texts by eye alone, can have little idea of the emotional involvement of a primitive audience under such conditions. This
point is well developed by Mrs. W. Muir in her book *Living with
Ballads*. The oral ballad tradition has survived in the Highlands
of Scotland down to our own day, and Mrs Muir has had
experience of it. Describing the technique and impact on the
audience of a famous female singer, she says: 'The singer's
voice is quite impersonal – she is merely the vehicle through
which flows a remarkable sense of duration, almost of inevitable ceremony and ritual. The slow build-up works on one's
feelings well below the level of consciousness'.** It is clear that
under such conditions the hearers are almost literally spell-
bound by the magic of the tale; they are more participants in
a ritual than hearers of an entertainment.

    9. We are to imagine, then, a singer who has been
called on to relate some part of a well-known legend. He has
in his mind at least the outline of the story; the known pattern
of the hexameter forms a fixed frame within which he will
compose; certain thematic passages are already fixed in his
mind; in addition, he knows a wide range of phrases, partly
handed down by his predecessors, partly perhaps invented by
himself, which will fit the characters and situations which he
will have to describe. For example, in *Od. i.* 3 the line ends with
the words '*Ŏdŭssḗŏs phĭlŏs hŭiŏs*' – 'the good son of Odysseus' –
and this is a standard way of describing Telemachus. However,
if the sense of what had previously been said had occupied one
more syllable in the line, the poet would have described the
young man as '*Tēlĕmăchŏs thĕŏeídēs*' – 'Telemachus the

* E. A. Havelock, *Preface to Plato*, ch. ix (cf. Bibliography).
** Willa Muir, *Living with Ballads*, p.46 (London, 1965).

god-like'. Elsewhere we find '*Tēlĕmăchŏs pĕpnúmĕnŏs*' – 'Telemachus the shrewd', a phrase which the poet would find convenient after the first foot of the line. In general, it is true to
say that such formulae are not interchangeable; where there
is more than one noun-plus-adjective phrase available in the
bardic repertoire to describe a single object or person, each
version fits one position in the line and one only. The poet
does not choose the formulae which he prefers, but selects the
only one which the metre at that point permits.

10. In view of all this, the reader may well wonder
how far any originality at all can be ascribed to the oral poet.
It is clear that there is in the Homeric poems much less sheer
invention, whether in the story or in the words, than we
should expect from a modern novelist. As has been shown, a
large part of the diction is formulaic, and a large part of the
story either traditional or thematic; exactly how much we
shall never know, but certainly more than half. And yet the
Odyssey has retained a freshness which makes it popular even
after nearly three millennia and even in translation. In the
case of the particular passages which follow, detailed reasons
are suggested in the appreciations; but in addition there are
some general points which may be made.

11. First, it is possible to construct a new building
out of re-used material. It may be that much of the text of
Homer is constructed from 'other men's flowers', but the poet
may nevertheless have made it entirely his own. For example,
it seems likely that the character of Nausicaa in Book *vi.*
(cf. Passage VI) may in origin be a figure from the common
bardic stock – the beautiful young princess who is destined to
marry the handsome shipwrecked stranger. But Homer has so
twisted this fairy-tale theme to suit his grand design that we
are hardly conscious of its ancestry, even though a close
scrutiny may reveal the points of junction with the main
fabric; and the girl herself, though described in standard
phrases, has a freshness which never fails to hold and amuse
the reader.

12. It may be true that, so long as the poet has a sharply-focused vision of both plot and characters, the formulaic and thematic techniques bring positive advantages. The audience is committed to the tale, yet for a good deal of the time its participation, though complete, is at a fairly low level of intensity; but when something really fresh is offered (and one suspects that such passages are often Homer's own, as in the 'island magic' lines of Passage II), there are ample reserves of emotional power both in the singer and in the audience. This is particularly true of characterization; no doubt the 'wily Odysseus' is in some degree a stock figure, but Homer has gone so far in depicting his versatility, endurance and adaptability that a genuinely living character confronts us, and one so strong that he has reappeared times without number in European literature from Sophocles to James Joyce.* This effect is, however, by no means confined to characterization, and the ability of even descriptive passages to 'come alive' is something quite remarkable and perhaps beyond the reach of analysis. It may be connected with Homer's habit of dealing in situations which have a strong appeal to basic human emotions, so that the combination of a spare but familiar diction with a critical moment in the plot has the effect of turning a key in a lock.** The door is opened and the reader, rather to his surprise, finds himself at large in the world of the imagination. It would seem that, for this particular effect to be obtained, the crisis must be described in this kind of language. We find an example in the Authorized Version rendering of the story of Rebekah at the well***, where we see a moment of vital importance for the family tree of the whole Jewish race. Abraham's steward has gone to the city of Nahor in search of a bride for his master's son, and he waits outside the city by the wall at evening:

* Cf. W. B. Stanford, *The Ulysses Theme* (cf. Bibliography).
** Cf. Passage XV, Appreciation, 9.
*** *Genesis*, 24, 15-18.

'And it came to pass, before he had done speaking, that, behold, Rebekah came out . . . with her pitcher upon her shoulder. And the damsel was very fair to look upon, a virgin, neither had any man known her; and she went down to the well, and filled her pitcher, and came up. And the servant ran to meet her, and said, "Let me, I pray thee, drink a little water of thy pitcher." And she said, "Drink, my lord"; and she hasted and let down her pitcher on her hand, and gave him to drink.'

Everything here is Homeric in feeling. The descriptions are formulaic ('a virgin, neither had any man known her'); the restraint is marked, and there is no attempt to play on our emotions, which are nevertheless deeply engaged. Finally, every detail bears its part, and several of them contain a 'hidden insight'; for example, if Rebekah 'went down to' the well, it may have been underground, as at Jericho and in mediaeval Orvieto; and the phrase 'she let down her pitcher upon her hand' shows us Rebekah carrying the water-pot either on her head or on her hip; she must lift it down if Abraham's steward is to drink. So little is said, and so much is conveyed. Where the style is so taut, the precise words used are vitally important, and this explains why in some modern versions of the Bible the narrative spell is so disastrously broken.

13. There has been a good deal of argument as to whether a 'stock epithet', which in some ways resembles the Wagnerian *leit-motiv*, may carry a more than conventional meaning on certain occasions, particularly if the normal sense is contradicted by the context. Thus, if the ground in which a man is buried be described as 'life-giving'* (the normal epithet for soil), are we to think that the poet intended an ironical contrast? It is admittedly difficult to say precisely how one is to recognize this kind of usage, but the reader will

---

* As at *Iliad iii.* 243.

find instances in the commentaries where it does seem that such a thing is happening.* As Maggie Tulliver says in *The Mill on the Floss*, 'If we use common words on a great occasion, they are more striking, because they are felt at once to have a particular meaning, like old banners, or every-day clothes hung up in a sacred place'.*** It does not of course follow that the original audiences were always aware of the true force of such epithets. Like a stimulating teacher, the bard offered more than most of his audience would consciously absorb.

14. It is important not to suppose that Homer's poetry is in any real sense 'primitive', or that because bards extemporized, their work was for that reason less finished than would be the case with a writer. This is not so at all. In fact, in one sense a 'revision' takes place every time a poem is sung. The poet, as he sings, is testing his skill against the reactions of his audience; failure, if it occurs, may be due to their boorishness, but it is just as likely to be due to his own errors, and it seems likely that the best bards were continuously improving both the details of the story and also the diction to be used. We know that there were many centuries of bardic singing behind the texts which we now attribute to Homer, and it follows, if what has been said above is correct, that our text is the result of a very long process of polishing and refining. How much of this work was due to Homer himself we simply do not know; it is in the places where the poetry is least evidently formulaic that one would begin to seek the poet's personal touch. Among the formulae themselves there may indeed be some of Homer's own making, but we have no means of discerning them.

15. This argument does not of course imply that the Greek text of Homer is in a state of unblemished perfection. It would be a miracle if over nearly three millennia a text of this length had been transmitted in a faultless state. But the poem as Homer composed it was no piece of extemporization,

* See Index under Epithets, active.
** George Eliot, *The Mill on the Floss*, Book VI, ch. 2.

being, in fact, the definitive version of a tale which had been growing to its maturity over a very long period. If there are errors they will be either in matters which circumstances made it hard for Homer to correct, as in descriptions of items of equipment which had become obsolete by the poet's own day, or else they will be due to miscopying, interpolation, omission and all the other dangers to which a hand-copied text was always liable.

16. To conclude: Homer's poetic style is extremely deceptive. The English reader who comes to Homer as part of his Greek studies begins by thinking that the *Odyssey* and *Iliad* are difficult poems. This is because he has usually started with fifth-century Attic Greek, and consequently he has trouble with the very different syntax, vocabulary and word-forms of the language in its earlier days; for Homer stands in relation to fifth-century Attic somewhat as Chaucer stands to Shakespeare. Once these obstacles are surmounted, there is a tendency to suppose that, because of the formulae and 'stock passages', Homer's Greek is idiosyncratic but repetitive and therefore undistinguished. This is very far from the truth. What we actually have is a word-fabric which presents a superficial appearance of uniformity and repetitiveness, but which is, in fact, brilliantly alive. It is alive because it has been pared away until only the relevant remains, and rehandled by craftsmen until the surface glitters; yet it is almost always 'understated', so that the reader has freedom to fill in details from his own imagination. Homer's style is marvellously well adapted to his task. There is nothing in the heroic world which it is inadequate to describe, from the fury of the storm to the quiet rollers breaking by night on a mysterious shore, from the delicate beauty of Nausicaa to the brutal realism of Odysseus' revenge.

Twenty Passages

Telemachus sets sail

Odyssey ii
413-434 *(the final lines of the book)*

Introduction

The goddess Athene has appeared to Telemachus, disguising herself as an old friend of the family, and has encouraged the young man to undertake his first adult exploit, a trip to Sparta (Lacedaemon), where he is to seek news from King Menelaus about his father, Odysseus, who is still absent from home after almost twenty years.

Translation

So Telemachus spoke, and led the way; the others went too. They carried all the gear and stowed it in the well-benched ship, as Odysseus' good son instructed. Up into the ship climbed Telemachus, with
5   Athene in front of him. She sat down at the stern and Telemachus beside her. The men let go the stern-cables; up they climbed and sat on the thwarts. Grey-eyed Athene sent them a following wind, a pure westerly, rippling over the wine-dark sea.
10   Telemachus gave the word, telling his men to seize the sheets; they did as he said. They raised and set the pinewood mast in its hollow step, fixed it with the forestays, and dragged up the white sails by their ox-hide thongs. The wind puffed into the
15   middle of the sail and the heaving* swell gurgled round the cutwater as the ship moved. She ran through the waves, cleaving her way. Then they made fast the sheets in the swift black ship and filled beakers to the brim with wine. They made
20   their libations to the immortal gods who are born for eternity, and especially to the grey-eyed daughter

* The meaning of the adjective is uncertain. It might alternatively mean 'glowing' (sc. in the sunset).

22 of Zeus herself. The ship, then: all night long and through the dawn she was making her way.

Appreciation

1. In this passage, composed largely of formulae, we feel the steady movement of traditional verse as the bard works his way, with assured control,* through a stereotyped pattern of events. We see the departure of any Homeric ship on any voyage; only the presence of the goddess distinguishes it from other similar occasions. There are, however, a few vivid touches; the wind 'ripples' over the sea in a line (Gk. 421)** where the participle *keladonta* gives the sound, and the metre being fully dactylic, is light in movement; and later, with these words

stéirē porphŭrĕŏn mĕgăl' éiăchĕ nĕŏs ĭoúsēs

(Gk. 428),

the repeated sounds of *s*, *ph*, and *ch* give the hissing of the prow as it cuts through the water. The sheets can be cleated because the weather is settled; once under way, the ship will not need any adjustment to the set of her square rig.

2. For the modern reader three main effects are noticeable:

a) The neutrality of the diction is appropriate for a 'bridging' passage. Telemachus has embarked on his mission, and now we are given a few moments in which to reflect on the difficulties of his situation and on the need for him to prove himself a true son of his father. The continued presence of Athene, who is not content with encouraging Telemachus in his own home but actually goes with him on the voyage, as she is later to stand by Odysseus at the killing of the suitors, affords good reason for hoping that all may turn out well in the end. It was an

---

* Even though there is some roughness of a type often found in Homer: e.g., the almost meaningless but metrically convenient particle 'ara' is found four times in as many lines.

** Line-references to the Greek text are thus designated for the benefit of those who have a line-by-line text either in Greek or English (cf. Bibliography).

important advantage of formulaic narrative that in such passages as this, instead of being insistently driven on by the complex detail of the narrative, as in a modern novel, the hearers were given time, by the occurrence of well-known 'stock passages', to turn over in their minds the significance of what had already been put before them. The bard also gained a useful rest during which he could look ahead to the next scene.

3. b) The result is that we see a picture of the daily life of the Homeric world which lies behind the immediate story. As C. S. Lewis has said, it is the distinguishing mark of a great epic poem that its 'imagined world must have a consistency and vitality which lay hold of the mind . . . It should remain with us as a stubborn memory, like some real place where we have once lived – a real place with its characteristic smells, sounds and colours: its unmistakable and irreplaceable "tang".'* The formulaic detail of such a passage as the one before us helps us to imagine the ordinary every-day world of ships, agriculture, 'seed-time and harvest, cold and heat, and summer and winter, and day and night'. Behind both *Odyssey* and *Iliad*, but more particularly in the case of the less warlike *Odyssey*, we are conscious of the normal background against which the great adventures are presented; and it is the quiet language of the 'stock' passages which most helps the imagination to take this in. A parallel effect is obtained in the *Iliad* by the use of frequent similes from daily life.

4. c) It is worth drawing attention to what one may call the 'zoom-lens technique' of the last line. Homer habitually varies his distance from the object described; he may be closely involved, or he may be looking from further away. Throughout Book *ii.* he has been giving us a detailed narrative designed to introduce us to Telemachus. The present passage, with its generalized picture of embarkation, slows the pace of events almost to a standstill. Finally, with the last lines of the

---

* C. S. Lewis, *Arthurian Torso*, p.190 (Oxford, 1948). For a different approach, see also E. A. Havelock, *Preface to Plato*, pp. 82-4 (cf. Bibliography).

book, the poet drops into the 'continuous imperfect' tense ('They were pouring libations', 'the ship was running'); the picture has become almost a 'still' as the camera moves back and away, so that we are left with the timeless image of a small sailing-boat which, having picked up the evening breeze from the islands to the mainland, is now sailing through the night and on into the dawn, apparently at the mercy of the elements, but actually guided and preserved by Athene herself; the scene is in a sense symbolic of the destinies of all Homeric heroes.

5. Formulaic narratives ('stock passages') are not always of this type. More often they are mere necessary links in the story-chain, as for example at *Od. iii.* 477–497, where Homer simply wishes to move Telemachus and Pisistratus from Pylos to Sparta.* The descriptive lines on that occasion are quite objective and do not seem to have any overtones. It may perhaps be objected that if in all these cases the language is similar, the decision as to whether a given passage is 'meaningful', as in the case we are now considering, or 'uncommitted', as at *Od. iii.* 477–497, must be subjective and arbitrary. In fact, however, this would only be true if each passage had to be considered in isolation. When one is reading the poem as a continuous narrative, it is generally clear whether the poet is using a given passage in any kind of symbolic way or merely as a necessary bridge between two incidents.

* Cf. also *Od. xv.* 282-300, where the return of Telemachus from Pylos to Ithaca is described in a shortened version of Passage I; the effect there is quite different, partly because of the shortening and partly because of other changes.

II

Island magic

(a) Odyssey v. 55-74

Introduction

At the beginning of the book, Athene succeeds in persuading Zeus to allow the release of Odysseus from his captivity on Calypso's island. Consequently Hermes, messenger of the gods, is sent down to take this command to the nymph.

Translation

When Hermes reached this distant island, he skimmed up from the dark blue sea onto the dry land and went on till he reached a big cave, the home of the long-haired nymph; and he found her inside. A big
5   fire was ablaze on the hearth, and far away across the island the scent of burning cedar and citronwood was wafted. Calypso herself was at her loom, going backwards and forwards with golden shuttle; she was singing, and lovely was her voice. Round the
10   cave stood a thicket of tall trees – alder, poplar, and scented cypress. There the long-winged birds would nest: owls, hawks, and the long-tongued cormorants, salt-water birds who busy themselves out at sea. Around the deep cave was stretched a luxuriant vine, heavy with grape-clusters. Springs, four of
15   them, one after another, were running with clear water; their sources were near together, but they trickled off in opposite directions. All round, soft meadows were thick with violets and wild celery.
20   Even an immortal, happening on such a place, might well gaze, and marvel, and feel delight in his heart.

5

(b) *Odyssey x. 210-223*

Introduction

Odysseus, at the court of King Alcinous in Phaeacia, is in the middle of the story of his wanderings. He tells how, with only one ship left, he sailed from Laestrygonia to Aeaea, the island of Circe, and here describes what happened to a reconnaissance-party.

Translation

In the woodland glades they found the halls of Circe, fashioned with cut stone, in a conspicuous* spot. Around it were wolves of the mountain and lions which she herself had tamed after giving them
5   unnatural drugs. The animals did not attack the party but stood up fawning with their long tails. These wolves, powerful of claw, and the lions too, were tame as dogs which fawn on their master as he leaves the banquet, knowing that he always brings
10   scraps to delight them. They fawned on the men, who were afraid at the sight of such strange creatures and stood still in the forecourt of the long-haired goddess; meanwhile they kept hearing the lovely voice of Circe as she sang indoors, going up
15   and down at her huge loom, fit for an immortal; for the weaving of goddesses is fine and delicate, a thing of glory.

Appreciation

1. It has sometimes been thought that the episodes of Circe and Calypso are 'doublets'; that is, that Homer had a single exemplar for the theme of 'enchantress on her island', but used it twice over. This may perhaps be true, but a close examination of the two passages here printed will show that the whole feeling of the two episodes is entirely different.

* The meaning 'sheltered' is also possible, but less likely. (The word does not occur often enough for us to be sure of its meaning).

Both are indeed intended to evoke a sense of the magical, but Calypso's home is described in language which is either neutral or favourable, whereas Circe's setting has always a suggestion of the black arts. The means by which the two passages, at first sight so similar, are so differently coloured, deserves examination.

2. Calypso's home, in an island whose name in Greek (Ogygia) is suggestive of great antiquity, is a cave, and there is a fire blazing; the scent which comes from it is a natural one. There are trees all round, and this general picture is brought into sharp focus* by the fact that the species are named. Birds roost in the trees, and they too are named; their long wings and long tongues add pictorial detail. Vineyard, running water, and flowering meadows complete the scene, at the centre of which we see the nymph singing. (The Greek word is ἀόιδῐᾰοῠσᾰ, with only two consonants to six vowel-sounds). It is an idyllic scene which conjures up Isaiah's phrase 'They shall not hurt nor destroy in all my holy mountain'.** Homer is using an extreme superlative*** when he says that even an Olympian might admire such a scene, and that Hermes paused to gaze at it. (*Od. v.* 75–6). It is in fact an earthly paradise, a wild-wood version of the garden of King Alcinous (see Passage VII).

3. The techniques by which this effect is obtained are noteworthy. The opening lines are neutral, and the adjectives in particular are formulaic and 'inert'. Thus the island is 'distant', the cave is 'big', and on the hearth a 'big' fire is blazing. It is only as the camera comes closer and the details of the setting are given that we begin to feel any power in the description. The 'golden shuttle' distinguishes Calypso as a person of wealth: the birds have their precise and pictorial epithets; the four streams and the meadows full of violets and

---

* Cf. Passage XVII, Appreciation, 4; and for another example of 'surface detail', see *Od. xix.* 225-235 (description of Odysseus' clothing).
** *Isaiah*, 11, 9.
*** Cf. Passage XVI, Appreciation, 4.

wild celery complete the scene in a highly individual way.*
There is nowhere else in the world of Homer which is quite like
this.

4. The metrical structure also is interesting. The
first eight lines are enjambed, which compels one to consider
them as a unit. Thereafter we are dealing with a 'miniature
catalogue' and can feel for ourselves how attractive such lists
can be, at any rate when they are on a small scale (cf. Passage
XX (b)). In this section the lines are mostly end-stopped, and
at one place we can see how easy it was for the oral bard to
expand or contract his episodes. 'Owls, hawks, and long-
tongued cormorants' says Homer, filling one line:

skṓpēs 't' īrḗkēs tĕ tănŭglṓs̀sōi tĕ kŏrónāi

Then he adds 'salt-water birds, who busy themselves out at
sea'. These words form another complete hexameter; if it had
been omitted, we should never have noticed its absence. As a
matter of fact it is the weakest line in the passage, for it adds
nothing to the picture, which would perhaps be better (because
denser) without it; we are not really interested in what these
birds do on other occasions.**

5. Circe's hall in (b) is no less vividly drawn, but the
tone is quite different. This is no rustic cave, but an enchantress' palace. Around it are wolves and lions, creatures harm-
ful in themselves and here depicted as drugged and charmed
into subjection. Their long tails create a very different picture
from the long wings and tongues of Calypso's owls, hawks, and
cormorants. These swishing tails are sinister, and the sight of
carnivores fawning,*** like house-dogs begging for scraps,
might well inspire fear in Odysseus' men. Circe is singing
and weaving, as Calypso was, and the formulae used are the
same,**** but now that we have taken in the colour of the

* Cf. Index s.v. Pictorial detail.
** Cf. Index s.v. Generalization.
*** The word, three times repeated, is even more emphatic in the Greek by
reason of its placing.
**** Though the participle 'singing' is here less vocalic (*ăēidóusēs*) than in the
case of Calypso (*ăŏidĭăoŭsă*).

scene, we know at once that Circe's song is as dangerous as Calypso's was innocent, and that the great web she is weaving, full of divine power, is more a spider's web than a housewife's. There is no echo here of Penelope at her loom.

6. It is noteworthy that the poet can achieve these two very differing effects in describing two very similar scenes, and it seems that the hearer must be sensitive to each phrase as it occurs. As soon as we hear of wolves and lions, the emotion of fear is lightly touched on, and everything which follows reinforces this feeling. The poet, usually withdrawn and refraining from moral comment, tells us plainly that Circe's drugs were unnatural, not beneficent. The men's fear is an inevitable consequence; they are after all human, whereas Hermes in (a) was protected by his divinity against earthly witchcraft. By this time a mood has been fully established, and it does not matter that the following lines are entirely neutral: the sense of fear continues and colours the feelings of the audience until such time as the bard strikes a new note. It is therefore very important to feel the mood of the poem as each section develops, because a tone developed early in the scene will predominate. This is a characteristic of Greek linguistics in general; the subject of a sentence, for example, once it has been stated, dominates and controls all that follows until such time as a new agent is specifically introduced.

7. Mrs. J. Chittenden has suggested* that in this episode Circe represents that central Minoan cult-figure, the Mistress of Animals, and that Hermes, who protects Odysseus by giving him the magical and otherwise unknown plant called 'moly' (*Od. x.* 302–306), is a Hellenized version of that goddess' male consort – the only power in heaven or earth likely to be able to break her spell. Certainly the animals, reminiscent of those depicted on the Lion Gate at Mycenae and in many

* *American Journal of Archaeology*, LII, 1948, pp. 24 ff.

Cretan representations of the goddess, fit this hypothesis well. The suggestion is of literary as well as religious interest, because the fascination exerted by the passage may owe something to the extreme antiquity of the picture which is being presented.* Any one who has looked at Minoan seal-impressions and frescoes, with their pictures of griffins, snake-goddesses, and demons, may well feel that Circe's ancestry lies in that world and not simply in the poet's imagination. It is noticeable that the passage describing the animals contains few known formulae. This may seem surprising if the above suggestions are correct; but the theme is one which by its nature must have been used only rarely, and this may be a sufficient explanation.

---

* Cf. Passage VII, Appreciation, 1-3.

III

Storm at sea

Odyssey v. 291-298 and 313-332

Introduction

Odysseus has sailed from Ogygia in his home-made boat; now he is alone on the ocean and exposed to the wrath of Poseidon, who sees at this point his last chance to exact vengeance for the blinding of his offspring, the Cyclops.

Translation

So Poseidon spoke, and assembled the clouds; he troubled the ocean, grasping his trident, and brought up every blast of every kind of wind; with clouds he covered earth and sea alike. Out of the sky
5 loomed up the dark. Up came all the winds, east, south, the blustering westerly, and the north wind who is born of the clear upper sky, thrusting a huge wave before him. Then Odysseus' knees and his spirit gave way, and finally with a groan he spoke
10 to his own brave heart . . .

(Gk. 299–312 are occupied by a soliloquy)

As Odysseus spoke, a great wave arched, broke terribly, and drove at him; it whipped the boat round. Far from the boat Odysseus was hurled, and the tiller dropped from his grasp. The mast snapped
15 at mid-point under the dreadful blast that came from the mixed gathering of the winds. Far away in the sea fell sail and yard-arm. Odysseus himself was submerged a good while and could not surface through the onslaught of that terrible sea; the
20 clothes which the nymph Calypso had provided weighed him down. Finally he got to the surface and spat out the bitter salt; water was running in floods from the crown of his head. But even so he did not despair of his boat; he struggled through the

25 waves, grabbed at it, and sat aboard it as his only
cover against death. The big seas carried it along
with the current, tossing it hither and thither.
Think of thistle-balls in autumn; the north wind
carries them over the plain, the thistle-heads cling-
30 ing thick together. Just so the winds drove the boat
all over the sea. Now the south wind would toss it
for the north wind to play with, now the east wind
would leave it to the mercy of the west.

Appreciation

1. The poet is depicting the storm rather than the
man; it is the power of the elements which he constantly
stresses, partly by personifying the winds and underlining
their variety, partly by describing in detail the efforts produced by 'all the winds at play'. Odysseus can achieve nothing
against all this; his boat is dismasted, he is thrown into the
sea and it is all he can do to climb back aboard the hulk and
cling on as wind and water do their worst. It is noticeable that
Poseidon himself, the power behind the storm, is only mentioned briefly. This provides a marked contrast with Virgil's
technique in *Aeneid i.* 34–123*, where we see a great deal of
Neptune and of Aeolus, his vassal. Homer does not want
anthropomorphic figures at this point in his narrative, and
concentrates on a description of the elements. The simile of
the thistle-balls contributes much; similes are less common
in the *Odyssey* than in the *Iliad*, exciting correspondingly more
attention when they do occur, and furthermore this particular
simile is unparalleled in Homer. Other technical devices are
also employed. In ll.1–5** the poet abandons his usual line-by-
line technique with stops or pauses at the end of each hexameter, and gives us a number of overrun lines which by their
very structure depict the powerful tumbling effect of the
storm; and in a different way the monosyllabic word *nux* (=

* The closing lines of this are included under Passage XII.
** Line-references without any prefix (as here) refer to the translation above.

'darkness as of night'), coming unexpectedly at the end of a
line and immediately before a full-stop, gives a sudden jarring
effect. The opening lines describing wind and water are full of
sibilants and hard consonants:

> hós éipōn sŭnắgē nĕphĕlắs ĕtărắxĕ dĕ póntŏn
> chĕrsĭ trĭắinắn hĕlōn, pắsắs d'ŏrŏthúnĕn ắĕllắs
> pāntóiŏn ắnĕmōn, sún dē nĕphĕĕ́ssĭ kắlúpsĕn
> gáiắn hŏmōu kắi póntŏn; ŏrŏrēi d'ōurắnŏthĕn núx.

(Gk., 291–4)

At a later point in the poem (*Od. ix.* 71), where he is describing
another storm at sea, Homer gives us a similarly graphic line
to describe the wind tearing sails to shreds:

> tríchthắ tĕ kắi tĕtrắchthắ dĭĕschĭsĕn ĭs ănĕmóiŏ.

('the power of the wind tore it three and four times')

Again* at *Od. v.* 313–4 we find:

> kúmắ kắt' ắkrēs
> dĕinŏn ĕpessŭmĕnŏn, pĕrĭ dē schĕdĭĕn ĕlĕlĭxĕ.

('a great arching wave which attacked with power
and spun the boat round')

To read such lines aloud is to hear for oneself the 'surge and
thunder of the *Odyssey*'.

2. Odysseus himself, though kept in the background,
is given enough living detail for us to picture his situation; in
particular, the realism of 11.21–3 is vivid – so vivid indeed that
the imagination conjures up a good deal more than Homer
actually describes, for the significant details give us enough
to work on. The soliloquy is introduced by words which are
entirely formulaic but which remind us, by the phrase 'brave
heart', that Odysseus' vital powers are threatened; this is a
picture which is fully developed in Passage V. However, our
attention at this point is clearly directed to the storm.

* Cf. also Passage XII, Appreciation, 3.

13

Odysseus himself is a tiny figure almost lost against the background of the tempest.

3. The diction is not in itself abnormally elevated, though great force and intensity are sustained throughout. One notices particularly ll.5–8, where the winds are described in an ascending series; east and south have no epithets, west is simply 'blustering', but the north wind comes from the ether, the region of power, the home of the gods, and consequently he is described as 'thrusting a huge wave before him'. Lines 1–10 are almost entirely formulaic, while the rest are less demonstrably so, though there is no variation in tone.

4. It has often been observed that throughout his sea-wanderings Odysseus receives no help from Athene, who at all other points in the poem is shown as almost officiously ready to act on behalf of the hero or any member of his family. The ultimate reason for this fact may lie far back in the history of the composition of the poem; perhaps in a remote past this particular tale was told not about Odysseus at all but about some other mariner who had no divine patron. Thus when Odysseus does receive help in Book *v.*, it comes from a minor sea-nymph named Ino, who has in our story no motive other than pity for her action, and who has no further part to play. However this may be, it seems that Homer (who was after all perfectly capable of 'writing in' an intervention by Athene at this point if he had wished to do so) has chosen to show us Odysseus entirely alone and depending at this moment on his own unaided powers. He is presenting his hero not merely as versatile and clever, but also as a man cast in the true heroic mould, one who feels despair at the odds against him, but nevertheless goes on struggling. The ordeal by sea is the equivalent for Odysseus of the ordeal by battle which is undergone by the main characters of the *Iliad*.

5. If this view is correct, Homer is seen both managing the architecture of his poem with great skill, and also using an 'impersonal' technique of verbal composition, with a single end in view, namely that the hero may be seen struggling against, and surviving, the full force of the elements. Only when his heroism has been established in this way shall we feel it right to take an interest in his other qualities. Perhaps the word-order of the invocation in Book *i.* is significant:

ándră mŏi énnĕpĕ, Mŏusă, pŏlútrŏpŏn . . .

'*The man*, O Muse, tell me of the man of many devices'. It may well have been with this end in view that Homer adopted the sophisticated 'flash-back' technique, whereby the narration of the earlier part of Odysseus' wanderings, in which he has his men to support him, is deferred until we come to Phaeacia. When we first meet Odysseus he has been left alone to prove his quality.

IV

Cast ashore

Odyssey v. 424-450

Introduction

Forty-eight hours have elapsed since Odysseus was forced to leave his boat and swim for his life. Now he finds himself off the unknown coast of Phaeacia, and must somehow get ashore.

Translation

Just as he was turning this over in mind and heart, a huge wave was carrying him against a rocky shore. There he would have had his skin flayed off him and his bones smashed if the grey-eyed goddess Athene
5 had not put an idea into his head. He swam with all his strength to a rock, grabbed it with both hands, and held on, screaming with pain, till the great wave had passed over. That was how he escaped it. But the backwash hit him again with full force and
10 hurled him far out to sea. When an octopus is dragged from its lair, many pebbles stick to its suckers; just so with Odysseus – the flesh was stripped from those valiant hands as they were dragged from the rocks. Then the great wave buried him. Odysseus,
15 poor man, would have perished there and then, contrary to his destiny, if the grey-eyed goddess Athene had not given him a further idea. He got his head above the waves as they thundered in towards the mainland, and he swam along outside the breakers,
20 looking towards the shore, to see if he could find anywhere a shelving beach and a haven from the sea. As he swam, he came to the mouth of a river, nobly flowing; that seemed the best place, clear of rocks and protected from the wind. He could dis-
25 tinguish the fresh water as it flowed into the sea,

and he shaped a prayer in his heart:
'Hear, Lord, whosoever thou art; with prayers from
the soul I approach thee; a fugitive am I from the
threats of Poseidon. Even among the immortals
30 that man is to be respected who comes wandering,
as I do now. After all my labours I come to thy
waters, throw myself at thy knees. Pity me, Lord;
I claim a suppliant's rights.' Those were Odysseus'
words. The god checked the flow, held back the
35 rough water, created a calm before him, granted
him safe passage into the river's mouth. Odysseus
relaxed both his knees and those mighty arms; his
strength had been broken by the salt water. All his
flesh was swollen, and the sea-water welled up out
40 of his mouth and nostrils. There was neither breath
nor voice in him as he lay there at the end of his
powers, overcome by desperate weariness.

Appreciation
1. We notice first that, after a long absence from the
scene, Athene is again in evidence. In Homer, divine intervention may be of many kinds. On rare occasions there is an
actual interference with the course of nature, as when Athene
herself brings the fighting to an abrupt end in the final lines
of the whole poem. Sometimes there is a minor change in
circumstances, as in ll.34-6, where we do not have to think in
terms of a miracle. No doubt it was a miracle which Odysseus
was praying for, but it would be possible to rationalize the
event as a 'marked improvement in weather-conditions'.
Finally, we have the situation described in ll.4-5, where the
intervening deity neither appears in person nor interferes
with the course of nature but merely puts thoughts into the
mind. It is a striking fact that the first idea which Athene puts
into Odysseus' mind at this point does not seem to be a very
helpful one; it actually results in his losing the skin of both
hands and being hurled out to sea again. The second idea

however is one which Odysseus had previously rejected as impracticable (*Od. v.* 417–423). What we really see here is Odysseus using his own wits and saving himself by means of his own resources, and this illustrates the point that Homer, lacking full powers of psychological description and analysis, will often 'externalize' a sudden change of plan and describe it as something given to a character 'from outside'; and if from outside, then presumably from some divinity.

2. The ruthless realism which we saw in Passage III continues (for example, Odysseus is stripped from his rock and hurled out to sea like a mere piece of flotsam), but whereas in Passage III the interest centred on the external phenomena, here the reader feels intensely for Odysseus as the skin is stripped from his hands. Nothing is actually said about Odysseus' feelings, but we are made to share them by an interesting use of 'inverted simile'. Homer says that it was 'as when an octopus is dragged from its lair' with pebbles still adhering to its suckers; yet actually in the case of Odysseus the opposite has occurred. It is the skin of his hands which is left on the rocks, not the rocks which are pulled away by his hands. Yet the image of the squid with its sprawling tentacles is so apt for Odysseus as he lies there spread-eagled, and the final uselessness of the 'suction-pads' in each case is so clear a point of comparison, that we do not at first sight notice the inexactness of the simile at its central point. Two points of detail are of interest:

(a) The word for suckers (*kŏtŭlēdŏnŏphĭn*) has an archaic termination which makes one feel that the picture has come down from a remote past.

(b) The phrase 'valiant hands' (1.13), formulaic though it is, momentarily concentrates our attention on the point of focus; the tighter Odysseus' grasp, the more he suffers.

3. After this painful incident, Odysseus swims until he comes to the mouth of the river, which is described in a fully dactylic line (ll.22–3):

áll' hŏtë dé pŏtămóiŏ kătā| stŏmă| kállĭrhŏóiŏ

where the adjective *kallirhooio* ('nobly-flowing') is both pictorial and onomatopoeic. This theme of the beauty of big rivers is frequent in Homer, and different devices are used to bring out the flavour. For example at *Iliad xxi.* 8 we find

ēs pŏtămōn ēileúntŏ băthúrrhŏŏn argŭrŏdínēn

('They were bunched up in the bed of the river, deep flowing, with silver eddies'), where the two compound pictorial adjectives contrast the inherent qualities of the river Scamander with the blood and the noise soon to be described. Again at *Iliad xviii.* 576 we find the line

pār pŏtămōn kĕlădóntă, párā rhŏdănōn dŏnăkĕā

('Along the sounding river, beside the quivering reeds'), where the mere sound of the line irresistibly evokes the feeling of wind and water.

4. In the passage which we are considering, Homer perhaps intends a contrast between the gentle, ordered flow of the river and the wild fury of the storm at sea which Odysseus has just survived and which was so powerfully described in Passage III.

5. Finally, Odysseus' prayer is of interest. In Homer, all suppliants have rights, but they are not always observed. Thus in *Iliad xxii.* Achilles, provoked by his rage into disregarding the normal heroic code, spurns Hector's dying plea. In our passage, Odysseus makes his supplication as intense as it can possibly be; it is reasoned but passionate, because this, as he well knows, is his last chance. The reader wonders whether Poseidon in his anger will have the power to control this freshwater stream, obviously an inferior deity, yet twice addressed by Odysseus with the title of '*ánax*' ('Lord'), the highest known in Homeric society. The river-god, who remains strangely anonymous, answers the appeal (this is perhaps made possible for him by the fact that Poseidon has now left the scene –

cf. *Od. v.* 380–1), and the crisis passes. The distinction between the minor deity and the physical river is curiously uncertain; Odysseus appeals to 'thy waters . . . thy knees' (1.32), thinking simultaneously of the running water before him and of an anthropomorphic figure, as if it were a statue which he was worshipping.

6. So Odysseus drags himself painfully out of the water at last. Homer never describes the actual moment of landing, but focuses our attention on the arms and knees of this piece of wreckage on the shore – the barely-living remains of a man.

The seed of life

Odyssey v. 474-493
(*the final lines of the book*)

Introduction

This passage follows IV almost immediately. In the interval, Odysseus has duly returned to the water* the magic head-band of the sea-nymph Ino, and has considered his best plan of action.

Translation

As he considered, this seemed to him the better plan. He went in search of some woodland, and found it near the water, in a conspicuous place. He crept under a pair of bushes growing from a single stock, one a cultivated olive and the other a wild one. They were impenetrable to the powerful moist breath of the winds; the gleaming sun did not pierce them with his rays, nor did rain strike through, so thickly were they intertwined. Odysseus ducked under and busily piled up a bed for himself, a huge one; for there was a mighty great fall of leaves, enough to cover two or three men in winter-time, however hard the weather. At this sight the sufferer rejoiced, Odysseus of heavenly descent; he lay down in the middle and heaped up leaves on top of him. A man who lives far away from his neighbours at the limit of cultivation will cover a log with dark ashes, keeping the seed of fire alive, lest he may have to rekindle from another man's hearth. Just so did Odysseus cover himself with leaves. Athene poured sweet sleep to close his eyelids and give him immediate rest from his grievous labours.

* For this theme, cf. the story of King Arthur and his sword Excalibur.

Appreciation

1. Odysseus must now find shelter or die of exhaustion. Our passage remarkably conveys his success. The double olive-bush has no parallel in Homer (or perhaps in nature), and it is curiously memorable. The reader feels that he would recognize the spot; and indeed the whole of the description in this section of the poem, despite its generally formal character, conveys a vivid picture. The beach may be at any Mediterranean river-mouth, but Odysseus' total exhaustion and the particularity of his lair, with its 'babes-in-the-wood' feeling, combine to make the scene memorable. This effect of 'particularizing detail' is one at which Homer excels. We remember Nestor's account (*Od. iii.* 293 ff.) of the harbour of Gortyn in Crete; there the phrasing is quite general until we come to one bold detail: 'The south wind drives a heavy sea against a headland on the left, and a tiny rock keeps off the force of the sea'. Suddenly we feel ourselves to be on board a small ship entering that harbour and picking up the pilot's marks.

2. The cover provided by the thicket is like that of a wild beast's lair, and it is clearly from that theme that Homer has borrowed the lines. At *Od. xix.* 428 ff., where Homer is telling how Odysseus got his tell-tale scar (cf. Passage XVII), he relates the story of how Autolycus and his sons, in company with Odysseus, once attacked a wild boar in its lair on Mount Parnassus. The lair is described in four lines virtually identical with *Od. v.* 478–80 and 483. No doubt the use of this theme in our passage was partly a matter of convenience, but it is highly appropriate to Odysseus at this moment; he is indeed like a cornered animal.

3. The leaves (ll.11–20) are a mercy which Odysseus did not expect. There are interesting traces here of a double narrative. In l.10 Odysseus 'piled up a bed'; and in l.14 he 'lay down and heaped up the leaves'. This repetition has the effect of dwelling on the events described and making us feel their importance. There is also emphasis on the number of the leaves: the bed is a 'huge' one, and there is a 'mighty great pile'

of leaves (the phrase in Greek has a touch of the vernacular about it): Odysseus 'pours the leaves over him' so that he gets the maximum insulation. All this prepares us for the simile which follows. In Odysseus' urgent need for warmth we feel how near he has come to the end of his strength; and this in turn must enhance the admiration which we are intended to feel for his self-control in remembering to return the sea-nymph's veil to the water in accordance with her instructions.

4. The simile of the 'seed of fire' is one of the most telling in all Homer. The isolation of the farmer on the limit of cultivation corresponds to the loneliness of Odysseus, the solitary wanderer who has nothing to help him but his own wit and strength. The 'seed of fire' is exact for the flicker of life which is all that remains after Odysseus' battering out at sea. The word for 'seed' (*spérmă*) is the more striking in that, although it is common in later Greek literature in both the literal and the metaphorical senses, this is the only occasion on which Homer uses it. The idea that the farmer must do all this because, if his fire goes out, he will have a long walk to his nearest neighbour, evokes a picture of a very remote era in which fire is not kindled by flint or friction but must be brought, like an Olympic flame, already burning from the nearest source*. As so often, the scene is drawn from agricultural life, evidently the setting with which the poet is most familiar. The language of the simile is cumulative, so that a broad out-line is first given, and then the detail is filled in; the phrasing in the Greek goes as follows: 'As when a man – a log, in the dark ashes he hides it – at the edge of cultivation – no neighbours'. Some of this effect is due to the ability of an inflected language to delay the placing of a vital word until the moment when it will have the most effect.

5. Throughout the whole passage one feels the tex-ture of a style which combines formulaic diction (about two-fifths of the whole section is material used elsewhere by

---

* For 'fire-fetching', cf. the Icelandic *Saga of Grettir the Strong*, Everyman Ed., cc 38 and 74-5.

Homer in identical or very similar form) with a normally simple syntax and vocabulary, and then impresses itself on the reader's imagination by the use of an unexpectedly striking phrase or touch, such as the picture of the double olive-bush or the evocative 'seed of fire' which is really the key to the whole passage. And all the time the attention is charmed by the steady movement of the metre, repetitive yet infinitely varied, whose spell is so much stronger than that of prose.

Washing-day in Phaeacia

Odyssey vi. 85-147

Introduction

As Odysseus sleeps in his lair, we are introduced to the magical land of Phaeacia, where King Alcinous' daughter, the princess Nausicaa, is persuaded by Athene to take her attendants and deal with the family washing.

Translation

Finally the girls reached the river, a lovely stream, where the laundry was done all the year round. Plenty of clear water kept flooding up from below, enough to cleanse even the dirtiest things. There
5   they unyoked the mules from the cart and set them loose to nibble the sweet grass beside the eddying river. Down from the cart they pulled the dirty clothes, brought dark water from the deep pools, and began to tread the clothes vigorously in the
10 troughs, competing together. When they had washed them and cleansed away all the dirt, they spread them in rows along the shore of the sea, where the pebbles lay which the ocean kept washing up onto the land. Then they bathed, smoothed oil
15 over themselves, and took their meal on the bank of the river, while the washing lay out to dry in the sunlight.

When Nausicaa and her attendants had eaten their fill, they took off their headbands and began
20 playing ball; the white-armed Nausicaa led them in song and dance. She looked like Artemis, archer-goddess, as she goes over the mountains – over lofty Taygetus, maybe, or Erymanthus – rejoicing in the wild boar and swift deer; beside her play the nymphs
25 of the country, the daughters of Zeus who wields

the aegis. Meanwhile Leto, her mother, rejoices
greatly. Artemis is taller by a head than the others,
so that she is easily identified, beautiful though
they all are. So among her hand-maidens stood
30 Nausicaa, virgin untouched by man.

When the princess, after yoking the mules and
folding the fine clothes, was about to set off for
home, the grey-eyed goddess Athene had a further
thought – that Odysseus should wake up and see the
35 lovely girl who (so the goddess intended) was to be
his guide to the city of the Phaeacians. So then the
princess threw the ball towards one of her companions. She missed the girl, and the ball went into
an eddying pool. All the girls screamed loudly.
40 Noble Odysseus woke up, and as he sat there he
brooded in mind and heart: 'Alas, what land of living
men do I find myself in now? Are they violent, wild,
unjust? Or are they fond of guests and god-fearing
in heart? Strange! the sound of young girls shouting
45 reaches me – nymphs, perhaps, who live on the high
peaks of the mountains, by springs of rivers and
grassy meadows. Or am I in the presence of human
speech? Come, I will investigate and see for myself'.

With these words the noble Odysseus emerged
50 from the thicket. With stalwart hands he snapped
off a branch among the close-packed trees, to cover
his private parts. He went on his way like a lion
reared in the hills, who, trusting in his power, goes
on through the wind and the rain with his eyes
55 blazing. It is the sheep or cattle he is after, or the
fast-moving deer. He will even, at his belly's promp-
ting, approach a walled fold to get his teeth into
some sheep. Just so Odysseus, naked though he was,
had to go up to these girls with their long hair;
60 urgent need was upon him. All foul as he was with
salt, he seemed a grizzly sight to them. They shrank

away in all directions onto the spits of sand. Only
the daughter of Alcinous stayed, because Athene put
courage in her heart and took fear from her limbs.

65 She stood her ground, face to face with Odysseus,
who wondered whether to clasp the knees of this
lovely girl and then make his supplication, or to
stand off and simply beseech her with honeyed words
to direct him to the city and give him some clothes.

70 As he reflected, it was the second plan which appeared
best – to stand off and beseech her with honeyed
words; he was afraid that, if he clasped her knees, the
girl might be deeply angered.

Appreciation

1. The feeling of grace and sunlight which pervades
the first half of this passage has not been achieved by chance.
Everything in the description is directed towards one end.
The scene is idyllic: the banks of a fine river (cf. Passage IV,
Appreciation, 3) and the neighbouring beach with its sandy
spits and its pebbles, the sunshine, the ball-game – all these
help to produce a picture both homely and refined, which is
elevated by the long Artemis-simile* so that we feel a strong
interest in Nausicaa both as a person and as a princess. The
transition from mere domesticity to a more dignified level is
brilliantly managed. As late as l.39 we are dealing only with
a picnic enjoyed by young women of the Phaeacian court, at
which sun-bathing and ball-games follow naturally after work
and lunch. Yet by the end of the simile we are prepared for the
royal dignity with which Nausicaa meets the intruder.

2. There is also a very discreetly-handled erotic
undertone. Homer clearly intends a contrast between the
femininity of the palace party and the rude virility of Odysseus,
who is extremely conscious (cf. ll.66 ff.) that his motives may

---

* This simile is picked up in the speech of Odysseus (*Od. vi.* 149 ff.) – a good
example of Homer's sophisticated 'integrating' technique. It is also a 'superlative produced by comparison': cf. Passage XVI, Appreciation, 4.

be misinterpreted. Everything in ll.1–30 emphasizes the beauty of the place and of the girls; everything in ll.40–61 emphasizes the toughness of the hero. This cannot be accidental. It seems likely that in a version of the story which antedates Homer, the scene was designed as a meeting between hero and heroine, a delightful 'love-at-first-sight' encounter which was to end with 'They lived happily ever after'. Nausicaa herself has wedding bells in mind, as is clear from *Od. vi.* 66 and also from her directly expressed wish (*Od. vi.* 244–5) that Odysseus may stay in Phaeacia and marry her. For such a development the present scene would be an admirable opening. Homer evidently cannot bear to put it aside altogether, even though his story does not permit such a marriage. He therefore retains the episode and manipulates it to suit his own ends. This can best be seen at *Od. viii.* 461–8., where the budding romance is brought to an end with touching brevity and dignity. Nausicaa says: 'Farewell, stranger and guest: one day, in your own country, remember me; you owe me the price of your life'. And Odysseus replies: 'Nausicaa, God grant my home-coming! Then I would pray to you always as to a goddess, every day of my life – my life, which is indeed your gift to me, my dear'.

    3. Is there perhaps a touch of humour at 1.65 ff.? The situation would be embarrassing for a modern hero. It was certainly less so in the world of epic, where visiting heroes are regularly given a bath by the maidservants or even the daughters of the house.* Odysseus is not embarrassed; it is simply that his motives may be misinterpreted. He therefore deliberately sacrifices the weapon of suppliancy in favour of a brilliant oratorical appeal. The reader was perhaps intended to smile at this, as he certainly was at *Od. xiii.* 287 ff, where Odysseus, deposited on the beach of Ithaca by the Phaeacians, meets Athene in disguise and at once spins the first of several yarns concocted to cover his identity. Athene 'smiles and pats him,' complimenting him on his ingenuity; he is the best

---

* Cf. *Od. iii.* 464–5; *iv.* 49.

deceiver on earth, she says, just as she herself is in Olympus. All this is done in such a way as to transmit Homer's amusement.

Commentary

4. ll.1–10 There is here an example of awkwardness in the text which may lead us to think that the poet has fused two incompatible themes. At 1.3 the picture is of a powerful river; the washing will be done, one presumes, by rubbing on smooth stones, as often happens to this day in remote places. The force of the stream, 'flooding up from below', will do most of the cleansing. Yet at 1.8 the girls have to fetch water and the washing is done by trampling it in troughs; it makes no difference whether these are natural or artificial. The point in itself is of no importance, but the roughness of the detail demonstrates the existence of the alternatives.

5. ll.1–30 It is interesting that in this pleasant scene the tone is purely factual as we are led through the components of what must have been a well-known picture. No detail obtrudes, yet the whole as it unfolds has a curious 'Grecian-urn' quality. The charm lies in the adjectives. The grass (1.6) is 'honey-sweet', the water (1.8) is 'dark' (presumably because it comes from deep pools), the river (1.7) has one of the usual 'running-water' adjectives. The effect is as if we could see a painter at work filling in one part of the canvas after another; everything in the end is balanced, nothing intrudes or is distorted. The Artemis-simile changes the mood to something more elevated, and in 1.30 a conscious effect seems to be aimed at. An unmarried girl is regularly in Homer *párthĕnŏs ádmēs*, 'virgin untouched by man'; however in this context the effect is unusual, because the words come at the end of a paragraph and the adjective is placed, contrary to normal Greek usage, in final position before a full-stop. We know from *Od. vi.* 66 that Nausicaa has thoughts of marriage; by his emphasis here Homer recalls the fact to our mind and prepares us for the confrontation with Odysseus.

6. The formulaic style has the ability to build up a word-picture more effortlessly than is the case with later, more self-conscious writing. This is because the bard is not constrained to avoid repetitions and echoes, and these all help to construct a mood in the mind of the hearer. Thus in ll.1–17, where we are concerned with the scene on the banks of this kindly river which has befriended Odysseus, we find the following words and phrases, all connected with water: 'the river, a lovely stream – the laundry-place – plenty of clear water – the eddying river – water from the deep pools – the banks of the river'. Yet Homer is not actually engaged on a description of the scene, but is telling us about the process of washing clothes. The riverside picture emerges as a by-product of the narrative, and it is a mistake to read Homer's narrative, especially in the *Odyssey*, as if he were only concerned to tell the story of interesting people in interesting situations. No doubt that was what the audience chiefly wanted; but the poet gave them a great deal more.

The palace of King Alcinous

Odyssey vii. 78-132

Introduction

Helped by Nausicaa and advised by Athene, Odysseus finds himself outside the palace of King Alcinous in the island of Scheria.

Translation

With these words the grey-eyed goddess Athene departed over the unharvested sea. She left lovely Scheria and came to Marathon and to Athens with its broad streets, where she entered the well-built
5   house of Erechtheus. Odysseus for his part went on his way towards the glorious halls of Alcinous. Before he reached the brazen threshold, he kept checking his steps as amazement filled his heart. Over the high-roofed hall of noble Alcinous there
10   was a radiance like that of the sun or the moon. Brazen were the walls of the courtyard as they ran round in both directions from the entrance to the heart of the palace itself, and on top was a coping of lapis-lazuli. Golden were the gates that divided
15   it from the well-built palace within; silver the door-posts that stood on the brazen threshold, silver the lintel above, golden the door-handle. On either side stood gold and silver dogs, creatures deathless and ageless for eternity, which Hephaestus had created
20   with knowledge and skill to guard the palace of noble Alcinous. Inside, around the walls in both directions from the threshold towards the heart of the house, were placed thrones on which had been cast robes light in texture, beautifully woven, the
25   work of women's hands. There the lords of the Phaeacians would sit eating and drinking; the

supplies were inexhaustible. On finely-made plinths
stood golden statues of young boys with blazing
torches in their hands, giving light to the ban-
30 queters all night long. Alcinous has in his palace
fifty sewing-women, some of whom grind the ripe
corn with querns, while others sit and weave at the
loom, or spin off the yarn from the distaff; their
hands flicker like the leaves of a tall poplar. The
35 sticky oil drips from the close-woven fabric; for the
Phaeacian women are as skilled at the loom as their
menfolk are outstanding in their knowledge of how
to speed a swift ship over the sea. The women have
their skill as a gift from Athene; they are crafts-
40 women in fine fabrics.

Outside the courtyard, near the gateway, is a
great four-acre orchard, with a barrier all round.
In it grow and flourish tall trees – pears, pome-
granates, apples with splendid fruit, sweet figs, and
45 luxuriant olives. On these trees fruit is never lacking; it does not fail either in winter or summer,
but goes on all the year round. The west wind con-
tinually breathes on them and brings some on
while it ripens others. Pear after pear, apple after
50 apple, vine after vine, fig after fig – all mature in
succession. It is there that Alcinous' fruitful vineyard is set. In one area, the drying-ground lies full
in the sun in a level patch; in another the vintage
is being gathered; in a third they are treading
55 grapes. In front are the unripe grapes shedding their
blossoms, while another group are beginning to
turn colour. Here, beside the lowest row of vines,
lie ornamental flower-beds, colourful all the year
round. There are two springs of water. One distri-
60 butes its water all over the garden; the other, on
the opposite side, flows under the threshold of the
courtyard towards the tall palace. It was from this

63   that the citizens used to draw water. Such were the
      glorious gifts of the gods in the precinct of Alcinous.

Appreciation
      1. Odysseus stands in amazement before the palace
of King Alcinous, and we are surely meant to remember his
son's similar amazement at the palace of King Menelaus in
Sparta.* Quite apart from the general similarity, one complete
line occurs in both passages to describe the 'radiance' of the
palaces. It seems therefore that the comparison was intended.
Telemachus stood wide-eyed in Sparta, and this was a reaction natural enough in a young man who had never before
been away from home; if Odysseus, that much-travelled hero,
experiences a similar reaction in Phaeacia, we must imagine
that the palace of Alcinous is something grander by far than
anything previously described. What follows supports this
view. The whole movement of the story is halted for more
than fifty lines while Homer gives us a detailed account of
these wonders, among which are some things which deserve
further consideration.
      2. This palace is no mere elaboration of what Homer
gives us elsewhere. Almost everything about it is strange and
has a touch of the magical which is brought out by the words
used. The 'brazen walls' are of course not from the world of
reality; the abundance of silver and gold gives an impression
of prodigal wealth, reinforced by the repetition in emphatic
positions of the adjectives 'silver' and 'golden'; the statues
made by Hephaestus, though not actually described as self-
moving, are called 'deathless and ageless', which implies that
they are regarded as having certain lifelike qualities; and we
know from *Iliad xviii.* 373 ff. that Hephaestus had the ability
to make such robots.
      3. The establishment and skills portrayed in 11.30–40
are on a large scale, but they are not obviously superhuman:

* *Od.* iv, 71–5.

the simile of l.34 admirably gives us the rapid movement of many hands simultaneously at work. However, with ll.41–64 we are back again in a paradisal atmosphere. Alcinous' garden has advantages denied to ordinary Greeks: a climate such that there is a steady succession of crops of all kinds, and constant supplies of fresh water for irrigation. In all this it may be that Homer is simply inventing, but the picture which he gives us is remarkably sharp and clear, so much so that in the case of the garden, which is very formal in arrangement, it is almost possible to draw a plan of the lay-out. The overall picture of a great palace employing labour on a large scale and containing within itself vast resources of wealth, materials and skill, seems in fact to be an idealized picture of the great Mycenaean or, more especially, Minoan palaces. The elaborate store-chambers of the palace at Cnossus in Crete must have given the impression of a civilization so wealthy that only a continuous succession of crops, such as is described here, could have kept it supplied. This imaginary concept is worked on by the poet's imagination in terms of vineyards and orchards known to him, and the picture hardens into the theme of 'wealthy palace in days gone by'. In the end there remains something slightly naive and wide-eyed about the description, which is characteristic of Homer when he is working with material which lies beyond his personal range of experience.

4. The suggestion that we have before us a stock passage which has not been quite fully assimilated to its context is supported by the striking change of tense in the last three lines.* Up to l.30 all the tenses are past: we are looking at the palace through Odysseus' eyes, and the past tense is appropriate. In l.30 a series of present tenses begin and continue down to l.62, representing, one would suppose, an original eyewitness account. In l.63 we find past tenses again as the poet picks up the narrative thread; in the Greek the change

* For further comment see S. E. Bassett, *The Poetry of Homer*, pp. 88 ff. (cf. Bibliography).

occurs abruptly in the middle of a sentence, and the past tenses both belong to 'stock lines', the last being of a generalizing kind.

5. Between 1.41 and 1.64 there are also some other linguistic features which seem to point in the same direction. Some of the lines seem rather mechanical and are constructed without much care for detail. Thus in ll.43–5 some of the trees have adjectives, while others do not, apparently as a matter of metrical convenience. The whole sequence of repeated nouns in different cases ('pear after pear, apple after apple . . . ') is as monotonous in Greek as it is in English, and the effect is of a rather lumbering kind of composition. Finally the grammar in ll.53–5 is awkward. There is no means of demonstrating that all this comparative clumsiness is 'primitive'; it might just as easily come from the hand of a 'late interpolator', but in view of the suggestions made in the previous paragraph it is at least striking.

6. Precisely at the point where the change of tenses occurs (1.63) it may be possible to make a further deduction. The remark that 'the citizens drew water here' does not ring true. In the historical period Greek public fountains were placed, as they are today, in accessible places. Yet the orchard of King Alcinous was certainly not accessible to the public. In view of the change of tense which has already been discussed, it seems likely that Homer has truncated his description with a phrase applicable to his own day, and that his original went on to describe the interior waterworks of the palace. One of the most striking features of the palace of Minos at Cnossus was its extremely elaborate plumbing, complete with multiple water-channels and filter-beds, and one suspects that behind our description in ll.62–3 lies one which gave details of the miracles of the palace's interior plumbing. Homer chooses instead to abandon his exemplar at this point and return to the story of Odysseus.

7. If the foregoing interpretation is correct (and it must be emphasized that it is speculative) then the remarks made at the end of the Appreciation on Passage II are relevant here also. It would of course be helpful and valuable from an archaeological viewpoint if *Od. vii.* 78–132 could be regarded as representing, at however many removes, an eyewitness account of the great palace at Cnossus. A literary critic, however, will prefer to say that the passage is an extremely interesting one in its own right, and that the air of depth and solidity which underlies an apparent fairy-tale may owe something to a well-remembered legend of Minoan greatness. This is not unlike what happens to the readers of J. R. R. Tolkien's *The Lord of the Rings*,* where behind the imaginary account of the Rohirrim and Minas Tirith lies the author's deep knowledge of north European myth and saga. In each case a tale which is of itself both interesting and romantic gains in charm and credibility from the earlier stories and legends which can be dimly perceived in the background.

* London, 1954-5.

VIII

Landfall near Cyclops-land

Odyssey ix. 116-151

Introduction

Odysseus, urged by King Alcinous, has begun the story of his wanderings since the sack of Troy. He has told of a minor disaster inflicted on his crews by the Kikones in Thrace, and how he rescued his men from the sleepy charms of the Lotus-eaters. Now they reach the land of the giants, the lawless Cyclopes, where the adventure in the cave of Polyphemus is to take place.

Translation

'Now there is an island which lies outside the harbour, neither very near nor very far from Cyclops-land, a rough, well-wooded spot. In it are countless goats. All are wild, because there is no
5   coming and going of men to check them. Hunters, those scourers of the high hills who endure a life in the woods, do not visit the place, nor is it given over to sheep or ploughing; it has been, time out of mind, unsown, unploughed, unfrequented by
10   men; it is a pasture only for the bleating goats. The giants have no crimson-cheeked ships, and among them are no shipwrights to make well-benched ships which would visit the cities of men and conduct business for them, in the way that
15   ordinary people do cross the sea to visit one another. Such men would have made the island as fertile as the mainland; for it is no bad place, and would produce all fruits in their season. In it are meadows, well-watered and grassy, close to the shores of the
20   grey sea, and there would be rich vineyards. The ploughing would be easy, and they would regularly

37

reap rich crops in due season, as there is richness under the turf.

'In the island is a roadstead with safe anchorage;
25 no need there to throw out mooring-cables or lie to anchors fore and aft. No, you can beach your ship and stay till your men have a mind to move on and the winds are blowing in your favour. At the head of the creek flows clear water; it is a spring
30 rising under the rock. Poplars stand all round.

'That is where we sailed in, and a god must have guided us through the pitch-dark night; we could not see anything ahead. There was a thick mist round the ships, and no moon shining in the sky
35 above, which was all obscured by clouds. Not a man of us clapped eyes on the place, nor glimpsed the long rollers which we heard breaking against the shore, until the moment when the stout ships grounded. As they lay there, we had all the canvas
40 off them, and out we got onto the beach, with the sea lapping. We fell asleep as we waited for Dawn, the immortal one'.

Appreciation

1. This island deserves our attention. To begin with, it is described at greater length than its importance in the story seems to warrant; for in essence the place is hardly more than a convenient fiction, a spot where Odysseus' fleet may be left while he himself goes on with a single ship to encounter the Cyclops. Yet it is described in detail, with heavy emphasis on both its present wild state and its potential fertility. The Cyclopes, having no ships, cannot reach it, and thus, it is hinted, they will not be able to pursue Odysseus when he is fleeing; only the bleating goats (the adjective is onomatopoeic) make their home there. One feels that ll.1–23 are perhaps part of the description of an island which originally existed in the bard's repertoire for some other purpose, pos-

sibly as a place where castaways were destined to live for a while,* like the Swiss Family Robinson – castaways for whom the much-emphasized goats would have been an important item of diet. The 'retained' lines certainly give an attractive picture of a small Aegean paradise awaiting its possessors, but the tone remains factual and even didactic (cf. ll.14–15); it is potentially a good place, but hard work would be necessary for its cultivation. There are no romantic overtones, nothing of William Morris' 'place not made for earthly bliss/Or eyes of dying men'. There is also a slight awkwardness where the poet has failed to assimilate the passage to its context; thus it is difficult to conceive of the possibility of the giants sending 'men' (ll.12–17) to cultivate the island for them, for elsewhere in Book *ix.* there is no suggestion that they have human serfs. Perhaps the island did not belong to the Cyclops-story in the first instance.

2. The mystery deepens as we follow Odysseus' flotilla to its landing. The harbour** itself is accurately depicted, with its safe waters and the characteristic poplars, enlivened in this case by a clear spring, which sends a stream down to the beach at the head of the creek. Attractive though this is, it conjures up no one individual place; it is rather a characteristic setting for the special scene which follows (cf. Passage V, Appreciation). The silent approach in mist and darkness is emphasized, and perhaps the repeated '*ph*' and '*th*' of the Greek help this effect.*** These soft sounds are in marked contrast with what follows in l.37, where the regular beat of the waves is depicted:

óud' óun| kúmată|mắkra kŭlīndŏmĕnă prŏtĭ|chérsŏn|.

---

* It is noticeable that some of the phrases used here appear also at *Od. iv.* 354 ff., where Menelaus tells of an island off the coast of Egypt where he and his men were detained by contrary winds.

** For variants on the 'secret harbour' theme, cf. *Od. x.* 87-94. (Passage X) and *Od. xiii.* 96-112.

*** énthă, thĕos, ōrphnáiēn, prŏĕphắinĕ, bắthéiă, oūrănŏthen, prŏĕphắinĕ, nĕphĕĕssìn, énthă, óphthālmóisīn: there are 11 instances in 5 lines.

Here the coincidence of word-stress with first syllable of metrical foot underlines the effect. (Cf. Intro. 5–6.) This is followed by the actual beaching of the ships, where the rasp of keel on shingle is there (ll.39–40) for anyone who will stop to listen:

> . . . prín⎸néăs ĕ̆ussélmōus ĕpĭkélsai⎸
> kēlsă̆sésī dĕ̆ néŭsi . . .

The overall effect is extraordinarily evocative; the mysterious island, the divinely-guided approach: darkness and mist: the sound of the waves rolling in towards the beach: and, after disembarkation, the heavy sleep which overcomes the men as they wait for the dawn. The metrical effect of the last line is not to be passed over:

> énthă̆ d' ă̆pōbrí̆xăntĕs ĕmeínă̆mĕ̆ń Éō ⎸díā̆n

('we fell asleep as we waited for dawn, the immortal one')

The Homeric hexameter normally ends with a dactyl followed by a spondee ($-\underset{5}{\check{}\check{}} / \underset{6}{-}$) or a dactyl followed by a trochee ($-\underset{5}{\check{}\check{}} / \underset{6}{-\check{}}$). Occasionally, however, a spondee is substituted for the fifth-foot dactyl, as in the line we are considering.* The effect of this 'spondaic ending' is to slow down and dwell on the close of the line. In this instance we are meant to feel the length and quietness of the night, and this effect makes an admirable conclusion to a highly-wrought and mysterious picture.

    3. It is not altogether easy to understand the poet's purpose in giving us such an evocative passage at this point; for one can hardly doubt that there was such a purpose, even if the poet himself was not self-conscious enough to analyse his reasons. It is evident that Odysseus, from the moment when he sets sail from Troy at *Od. ix.* 39, has been gradually leaving the world of reality behind him. The Kikones (*Od. ix.* 39–61) have a place on the map. They are Thracians, and show themselves to be purely human enemies. The two-day storm which follows (*Od. ix.* 62–81) takes the flotilla southward to

---

* An alternative spelling of 'Eo' exists which would remove the effect.

Cape Malea, at the southern extremity of the Peloponnese. Thereafter we quit the real world and find ourselves in an area of romance and travellers' tales. The Lotus-eaters (*Od. ix.* 82–104) are apparently normal human beings, though their food is imaginary. The poet describes the incident in a matter-of-fact way, and goes on in a similar vein to a general description of the Cyclopes and their way of life (*Od. ix.* 105–115). Then follows the passage before us, which begins simply enough (ll.1–23) but ends with the mysterious and divinely guided arrival.

4. It would seem natural for the poet to give us a 'bridging passage' from the world of reality to that of romance, and the reverse transition is so marked at *Od. xii.* 78–92. (Passage XIII). Yet in our present passage the transition seems to come at the wrong point; we should have expected it before rather than after the episode of the Lotus-eaters.

5. We can only guess at a solution of this problem. It seems possible that what Homer actually gives us is not one but two bridging passages. In the first, the episode of the Lotus-eaters, we see how the world of unreality begins to break in; the scene itself is of a normal character, but some of Odysseus' men break down and lose one of the most deeply-implanted of all human instincts, the desire to return home, which Odysseus himself retains even under the most extreme pressure. It is only after showing us this psychological disintegration that the poet goes on to make the transition into a fully-imagined and fully-described world of fancy – a transition which we see before us in the second part of Passage VIII above. This time there is nothing about psychology; everything is externalized, and the effect of mystery is produced simply by a description of a strange landing at night, in which it is not the well-known figure of Athene who guides the ships, but an unspecified divine power which is all the stranger for being nameless.

IX

Fee Fi Fo Fum

(a) Odyssey ix. 287-293

Introduction

    The Cyclops has trapped Odysseus and his men inside the huge cave where he lives and keeps his sheep. Rejecting an appeal for hospitality, he has claimed not to be subject to human conventions.

Translation

'Those were my words; but the giant with pitiless heart made no answer at all. Instead, he leaped to his feet, set hands on my companions, grabbed two of them, and smashed them against the ground like puppies. Their brains ran out onto the soil below and soaked the floor. He jointed the corpses and got ready his meal. He ate like a mountain lion, never pausing – brains, flesh, and juicy bones.'

(b) Odyssey ix. 371-397

Introduction

    Odysseus plans to blind the Cyclops with a baulk of timber, and with this in mind drugs him by means of a triple helping of strong wine, in return for which the giant promises to eat him last of all.

Translation

'So he spoke, and fell flat on his back; then lay there, his huge neck twisted. Sleep, to whom all must yield, overcame him. Up from his throat gobbed wine and scraps of man-flesh. He belched from a
5   stomach heavy with wine. I pushed the stake under a heap of ashes to get hot, and spoke encouraging words to my companions in case any should panic and draw back. As soon as the olivewood stake in

the fire was on the point of bursting into flame, –
10   green timber though it was, it glowed terribly – I
brought it out from the fire, near the giant, and my
companions stood round. Some deity gave them
more than ordinary courage. They took the olive-
wood spit, sharp at the point, and jabbed it in his
15   eye. I myself pressed on it from above and twirled.
It was like the moment when a man is boring a ship's
timber; the workmen set the drill in motion from
below with a band, pulling on each side, and the drill
keeps running. That was how we twirled the fire-
20   hardened spit, keeping it in the eye-socket, which
grew hot, with blood running round it. As the eye-
ball caught fire, the blast singed his eyelid* and eyebrow*, and the roots of the eye spluttered. When a
bronze-smith dips a great axe or an adze in cold
25   water, tempering it (for iron is strengthened by
that), there comes a great hiss; so the Cyclops' eye
sizzled round the tip of the olive-wood spit. He uttered
an enormous, terrifying groan, and the whole cave
echoed. We panicked and rushed off, while the giant
30   dragged out of his eye the stake, all bloody.'

Appreciation and Commentary

1. It is evident that Homer wishes to extract the
greatest possible effect from his account of the blinding of the
Cyclops, which has always been thought of as one of the high-
lights of the poem. The ingenuity and courage of Odysseus are
at their most impressive when matched against so vast an
adversary. The bard clearly intends us to admire the plan
which Odysseus devises for escape from an apparently hopeless
situation; but, in order to convince us, he must also make us feel
the extreme brutality of the giant, so that we shall not have any

---

* Plural in the Greek, despite the fact that the Cyclops has only one of each;
but this may not be significant. See note in W. B. Stanford's edition (cf. Bibliography).

feeling of pity for him at the moment of assault. (Pity is to come later, with the incident of the ram). This is all very well done, though the modern reader may feel that the blood-and-thunder detail of the actual blinding are excessive: an example, perhaps, of 'playing to the gallery'. Most of the narrative speaks for itself, but a few separate points deserve comment:

2. 1.(a)4 The Greek is remarkably effective. The Cyclops grabs two men; whom, if we follow the order of the words in Greek, 'like puppies, against the ground, he smashed'. The monosyllabic verb* *kopt*, coming at the end of its sentence, and standing as first word in a line and before a full stop, has the force of an explosion. The harsh gutturals and sibilants reinforce the effect of heartless brutality which is in any case inherent in the simile:

> *sún dě dǔŏ márˈpsās hŏsˈ tē skǔlǎkās pǒtĭˈgáiē*ˈ
> *kópt'*; *ēk*ˈ*d' énkĕphǎlōs chǎmǎdīs rhĕĕ*ˈ. . .

('He grabbed two of them and smashed them against 'the ground like puppies; their brains ran out onto the soil below . . . ')

3. 1.(b)2 'Sleep, to whom all must yield'. The adjectival phrase translates one Greek word, *pandǎmǎtōr* (lit. 'all-subduing'). This word appears formulaic, although it is in fact used by Homer only on one other occasion, at *Iliad xxiv.* 5, where Achilles, mourning for Patroclus, resists 'all-subduing sleep'. In both passages the word seems to be worth more than its face value (Cf. Intro. 13). It was an essential part of the plan that the Cyclops should be drugged with the specially potent wine which Odysseus so fortunately had with him, 'wine which maketh glad the heart of man', as the Psalmist would have called it; and that no less formulaic phrase, if it had been used here, would have produced a similar effect to Homer's *pandamator*. Sleep is universal; normally it brings release from fatigue and pain, but here it will have the opposite effect. Those who doubt whether formulae can ever be more

---

* Cf. Passage XI, Appreciation, 7.

than 'inert' are not paying enough attention to the context. If *păndămătōr* is 'inert' here, it is the only word in the immediate context which is not 'pulling its weight'.

4. *The Blinding*, ll.(b)13–30. The narrative of the blinding gets most of its force from the two similes, both of which are elaborate. In the first of them (ll.16–19) the choice of a dockyard as the setting helps to underline the size of the Cyclops. The drill in each case has to be a very large one to deal with a ship's timbers. English readers will think of Milton's picture of Satan's spear

> . . . to equal which the tallest Pine
> Hewn on Norwegian hills to be the Mast
> Of some great ammiral, were but a wand.
>
> (P.L. *i.* 292–4)

The Cyclops lies there in all his bulk like some great ship under construction, and to bore into such materials needs endurance: in the Greek we find (Gk. 384–5) 'he bores it with a boring-tool', where the double use of the same root-word helps the impression of assiduity. Both in the simile and in the narrative the operator stands at the point of risk. In both cases the drill is awkwardly placed and has to be energized from below. This simile, then, works at all levels and in all its details. In the second one the point seems to lie only in the great hiss which is heard when a large red-hot piece of metal is dropped into cold water.

5. There are as a matter of fact grave technical difficulties about the whole operation as Homer describes it, and these have been fully analysed by Prof. D. L. Page*. For example, it seems likely that, in an earlier version of the story, the spit was a metal one, for olive-wood cannot be hardened by burning, nor would it hold its heat. However, such details go unobserved by the reader, and still more by the listener; the description is so powerful that we are content to accept Homer's narrative as it stands. The more one thinks

* *The Homeric Odyssey*, ch. 1 (cf. Bibliography).

about the matter, the less likely is it that the Cyclops' eyelid and eyebrow would in fact catch fire, and the more certain does it seem that mechanically all this is impossible and that in any case the Cyclops would have reacted instantaneously and squashed Odysseus like a fly. But there is not much point in wasting time on the matter (we do not, after all, have extensive scientific data relating to one-eyed giants); the narrative itself, which presses on as tirelessly as the drill in the simile, overwhelms all such petty criticism.

6. 1.(b)26. 'iron is strengthened by that'. Even in his finest passages, Homer will sometimes find time for a generalization of this kind (Cf. *Od. v.* 67, discussed in Passage II, Appreciation, 4). Homer's audience must have known as well as we do that cormorants 'busy themselves out at sea' and that iron is strengthened by tempering. It is perhaps best to think of such generalization as an extended form of the 'inert' formulaic epithet, a momentary rest for both singer and audience. Icelandic saga also tends on occasion to be sententious.

7. The last three lines deserve special consideration. The Cyclops 'uttered an enormous, terrifying groan, and the whole cave re-echoed'. Lines 28–29 are composed of two formulaic phrases, each of which is extremely effective. The first is *smérdălĕŏn dĕ mĕǧʰ ōmóxĕn*, where the adverb *smerdaleon* has reference to something big and frightening and has a certain onomatopoeic effect. The same is true of *omoxen*, 'he groaned', with its long open vowels. In the second phrase, the echoes which reverberate in the confined space of the cave are a vividly-imagined detail. Then the panic experienced by the men, whose enterprise has so far succeeded beyond all reasonable expectation, is a natural reaction from the preceding tension; they cannot get far away, and the danger is by no means over. Finally we are left with the picture of the bloody stake, symbol of all that has happened so far in an exploit worthy of James Bond, but far more effectively narrated than that hero's achievements.

Disaster in a fjord

Odyssey x. 77-132

Introduction

After escaping from the Cyclops, Odysseus per-
suades Aeolus, the wind-god, to imprison in a bag all the winds
except the one which will take him home. Within sight of
Ithaca, he is betrayed by his men, who undo the bag under the
impression that it contains treasure. The flotilla is driven
back into unknown regions. Odysseus himself is still narrating.

Translation

'From there we sailed on with grief in our hearts.
The men's spirit grew weary with our irksome,
useless rowing, now that we no longer had favourable conditions. However, we sailed on for six whole
5　days and nights, and on the seventh we came to the
steep citadel of Lamos, distant Laestrygonia. There
shepherd hails shepherd as he drives his flock home,
and the one who is outward bound hears him and
replies. A man who needed no sleep could get double
10　wages there, once as an oxherd and once for tending
the snow-white sheep. Near together in that country
are the paths of night and day.

'We reached a fine harbour; all around, the rock
runs up sheer and unbroken on either side. At the
15　entrance, projecting headlands jut out facing one
another to form jaws, and the passage is narrow.
My captains all took their handy ships right
through, and they moored inside this trough of a
harbour, very close together. There was never a
20　wave, big or small, inside the roadstead, only a
shimmering calm. However, I alone kept my dark
ship outside, right away from the place, and tied
up to a boulder. I went up onto a rocky crag and

stood there. There was no sign of ploughing or of
25 human habitation; the only thing we could see was
smoke leaping from the ground. Then I dispatched
some of my companions to go and find out who the
men were that lived mortal lives in that place. I chose
two, and sent a third with them as herald. They
30 disembarked and went off along a well-made road,
down which waggons used to bring timber from the
high hills to the town. They met a girl, a sturdy
young woman, drawing water in front of the town;
she was the daughter of Antiphates, King of Laes-
35 trygonia. She had gone down to that fair-flowing
spring (its name is Artakie) because it was from
there that they used to get water for the town. They
accosted her, asking who was king of this people
and had lordship over them. She at once pointed out
40 her father's lofty hall. When they entered the noble
palace, they found the queen at home; she was as big
as a mountain-peak, and they loathed her. She
instantly sent for her husband, famed Antiphates,
to come from the market-place; and he contrived a
45. nasty death for them. He immediately grabbed one
of those three companions, and prepared his meal;
the other two made off in flight and got to the ships.
Antiphates set up a hue and cry throughout the
town, and the sturdy Laestrygonians, hearing it,
50 came up on all sides. There were thousands of them,
more like giants than men. They stood on the crags
and began pelting my people with man-sized rocks.
A terrible hubbub sprang up among the ships as
men were destroyed and ships smashed. The Laes-
55 trygonians carried off their grizzly banquet like
men spearing fish.

'While my companions were being destroyed
inside that deep-water harbour, I drew my sharp
sword from my thigh and slashed the cables of my

60 blue-prowed ship. I gave my orders instantly, telling
my men to put their backs into the rowing if we
were to get away. Fearing destruction, they all
sent up clouds of spray. With joy we escaped those
arching rocks and ran out into the open sea; at
65 least, my own ship did. The others all perished
there inside'.

Appreciation

1. The needs of the story force Homer to reduce
Odysseus' flotilla to a single ship, and with this in mind he
places the remaining ships in a trap where wholesale destruction is plausible. Laestrygonia is well conceived for this
purpose. It is a long way from Greece and inhabited by a gigan-
tic people living in a strange part of the world where there is
in effect no night, so that a man who needed no sleep could
earn double wages. The precise meaning in ll.11–12 ('Near
together are the paths of night and day') is disputed, but it
seems clear that Homer is describing a place like the 'land of
the midnight sun'. Nor is there any reason why we should
reject out of hand the hypothesis that we have here a re-
working of travellers' tales about the far North. This is not
to say that Mycenaeans had sailed as far as Norway, but only
that trade causes contacts and transmits information about
distant places. Baltic amber* was in use in the Aegean during
the Mycenean period, and Mycenaean *objets d'art* penetrated
at least as far as Britain; it is likely that those who traded in
precious objects passed on stories as well. There are a number
of small points in the text which can be made to support the
identification of Laestrygonia with Norway, but in the end
one is bound to admit that it is by no means certain.

  2. The only alternative to the Norse hypothesis is
to think of Laestrygonia as entirely imaginary, and it may
be that such obviously invented names as Antiphates ('con-

* Cf. Passage XIV. Transl. 1.67.

tradictor') support this view. When Homer's sources give him no help he tends to invent 'meaningful' names like those which are so common in Dickens. Thus in the Phaeacian episode many names of minor Phaeacian characters are clearly fabricated, and most of them, appropriately enough, have something to do with the sea.

    3. It is interesting to note how the grim setting, whether Norwegian or imaginary, is overlaid by Hellenic practices. The daughter of Antiphates is found, like Rebekah, drawing water at the well outside the town, and the well has a very Hellenic name; in the historical period we find a fountain called Artakie at the Greek town of Cyzicus in the Black Sea. Antiphates himself is busy, like any Athenian, 'in the market-place'. By these means the poet makes the outlandish Laestrygonians comprehensible to his audience. Antiphates and his people share some of the qualities of the Cyclopes: for example, gigantic size and the habit of throwing huge stones when provoked. However, they appear to have the normal complement of eyes. It may be that there is some contamination between the two episodes; at any rate it is certain that Cyclopes and Laestrygonians alike would be objects of loathing to Greek eyes, and indeed Homer says as much in 1.42.

    4. This brings us to discuss the execution and tone of the whole passage. Homer seems to be interested at this point more in the story than in anything else. The brevity of 'and they loathed her' illustrates the point. As has been noticed,* a moralist such as Swift would have gone on to give us detailed reasons for the loathing; Homer has told us enough for his purpose, and hurries on to describe the sinking of the ships – which, as we saw, was probably his main reason for including this episode in the first instance. The narrative is in fact very rapid throughout: for example, the embassy, after conversing with the king's daughter, is in the next breath described as being inside the palace; and we are never told how

* S. E. Bassett, *The Poetry of Homer*, pp. 229-30 (cf. Bibliography).

Odysseus learned what had happened.

    5. The execution in general lacks the conviction of the Cyclops-narrative, perhaps because the poet has exerted all his powers over the not dissimilar scenes in *Od. ix* and has therefore to some extent worked out this vein. The charm of Passage VIII is entirely absent. The deep-water harbour described there was a place of peace; this 'trough of a harbour' in Laestrygonia is entirely sinister. Even the 'shimmering calm' of 1.21 is seen at once by Odysseus as dangerous, so that he keeps his own ship outside. The 'sheer rocks' which run down to the water only make it easier for the Laestrygonians to send boulders down onto the ships below. The whole setting repels us, and forms a suitable preparation for the final disaster. As usual, it is Odysseus' foresight which preserves his own ship. We must not ask, for the poet does not permit the question, why, if Odysseus was so suspicious, he did not order his captains to follow his own example. This is simply the instinctive and deeply-ingrained personal 'canniness' which will in the end preserve him after all his men have perished through their own folly.

Scylla and Charybdis

Odyssey xii. 201-259 and 426-446

Introduction

Odysseus and his men, having escaped from Circe's power (Cf. Passage II (b)), continue their voyage. Odysseus, bound to the mast on his own instructions, has resisted the Sirens' song and their promise of knowledge of past and future; the crew, their ears blocked by wax, hear nothing. The perils of Scylla and Charybdis lie ahead. Scylla, the lesser of two evils, is dealt with in the first part; Odysseus will face Charybdis alone after the death of his companions, shipwrecked as a consequence of their sacrilegious butchering of the cattle of the Sun. Odysseus is telling his own story in the palace of King Alcinous.

Translation

'But when we were leaving behind us the island of the Sirens, I soon caught sight of spray and heavy seas, and I heard a dull thudding. My men panicked; the oars flew from their hands and all clattered
5   against the ship, forced by the water. She lost way now that the crew were no longer handling the sharp-bladed oars. However, I went through the ship and encouraged my companions with words as sweet as honey, standing by each man in turn.
10   "Friends, we're not by any means without experience of trouble. But this is no greater disaster than when the Cyclops cooped us in his hollow cave by the force of his power. Even then, thanks to my courage, advice and shrewd thinking, we made our
15   escape; and I expect one day we shall look back on this adventure too. Come now, let us all do as I say. Sit there on the thwarts and strike the waves of the sea with your oars; perhaps Zeus may grant that

we escape or avoid this present peril. Helmsman: my
20 instructions for you now – keep them in your heart,
for you control the tiller of the hollow ship. Keep
her out of this spray and surge. Head for the crag.
Don't let her creep over the other way, or you'll
put us at risk."

25 'Those were my words, and the men obeyed at
once. But I did not now mention Scylla, that deadly
bane; I was afraid they would panic, stop their
rowing and take shelter below decks. At that
moment I forgot Circe's dire command not to put
30 on my armour; I slipped on my fine gear, I grasped
my two long spears, and I went on deck, up in the
bows. That was where I expected Scylla, the rock-
monster, trouble-bearer for my companions, to be
first seen. Nowhere could I discern her, though I
35 strained my eyes as I scanned the whole face of the
spray-clad rock. We were sailing through the narrows, lamenting. Scylla was on one side; on the
other, that strange Charybdis terribly sucked in
the salt of the sea. Whenever she vomited it up, she
40 kept seething and bubbling like a cauldron on a hot
fire. High above us, the spray kept falling on the
tops of the twin crags. Whenever she sucked in the
salt of the sea, the whole interior seethed and lay
open: the crag resounded terribly, and the earth
45 below kept coming into view, all dark with sand.
My men turned green with fear. Fearing our doom,
we were looking towards Charybdis. But just at that
moment Scylla grabbed six of my men out of the
hollow ship – the best of the crew in skill and
50 strength. I glanced towards the ship and ran my
eye back over the crew; suddenly I caught sight of
hands and feet aloft as the victims were hauled up.
Horror-struck, they were loudly calling on me by
name; that was the last time I ever heard their

55　voices. When a fisherman on a promontory with his
long rod throws out food into the sea as bait for
little fishes, then casts his line with its rough ox-
horn protector, and finally takes the fish and
throws them gasping behind him – so my men
60　gasped as they were lifted towards the crag. And
there, in the opening of her cave, she ate them,
while they screamed and held out their hands to
me in their agony. In all my ordeals while I crossed
the paths of the sea, that was the most pitiable
65　thing I ever set eyes on.

* *

'Then* the West Wind stopped raging and roaring,
and the South Wind came up at once with trouble
for me. I was to go back again through the whole
length of grim Charybdis. All night I was carried
70　along, and as the sun rose I came to Scylla's crag
and to deadly Charybdis, who was then sucking
in the salt of the sea. ✝ reached up into a tall fig-
tree, squeezed myself against it, hung there like a
bat. Nowhere could I support myself firmly on my
75　feet: nowhere to stand – the roots were far apart,
and the branches, tall and huge, casting shadow out
over Charybdis, were high above me. I hung on
grimly, till she should belch out once more my
mast and keel. So they emerged; late it was, and
80　great my longing by then. At the time of day when
a man gets up to go home from the market-place to
his supper, after settling many disputes between
young heroes who are quarrelling in the courts –
that was the time when the timbers came up from
85　Charybdis and into my sight. I let my hands and
feet fall free, and splashed down just alongside the
great timbers, then got astride them and paddled

---

* For part of the intervening narrative, see Passage XII (a).

88   with my hands. The father of gods and men did not
let Scylla have sight of me; I should never have
escaped utter destruction.'

Appreciation
Discussion of Narrative Technique
   1. Homer has just depicted Odysseus as highly
successful in dealing with the peril of the Sirens; consequently
the self-assertive approach ('posturing', cf. Intro. 3) will be
the more acceptable to the readers, as well as being in accordance with the usual heroic code of behaviour. Odysseus has
evidently digested Circe's advice on the choice between two
evils, and has made up his mind in advance. As so often, his
ability to think ahead is shown as the crew's only hope of
safety. He wastes no words, but merely issues the necessary
orders, showing himself a decisive man of action.
   2. It would seem that in ll.29-30 we have an unnecessary detail. The tone suggests that Odysseus' disregard of
Circe's instructions will in some way prove unfortunate, but
in fact no such consequence is mentioned. It may be that in
another version of this tale the disaster occurred while
Odysseus was below decks, putting on his armour – with the
suggestion that, had Odysseus been available, he might have
effected a rescue.* In our narrative he is actually on deck at
the time, but his attention is distracted by the sight of the
maelstrom of Charybdis. This is described in graphic but
exaggerated detail, with a technique which shows great command over pictorial effect. It is noticeable that the details
about Charybdis are much fuller than those about Scylla; this
is because the latter was fully described in Circe's warning.
Both Scylla and Charybdis are strongly personified; this is a
tendency of the Homeric style, which usually avoids abstracts
of any kind. As far as Scylla is concerned, Homer now contents
himself with an awe-inspiring suggestion (1.35) of the sheer

* Alternatively in that version resistance may have caused unnecessary deaths.

rock-face where her cave is to be found. Released from the need for detailed description, he gives his hearers an unusual view from the deck of the ship looking upwards as the men are seized and carried aloft, calling on their captain for help. The pathos of the situation is emphasized by Odysseus' comments in ll.63–5, and by the simile of the fishes in ll.55–59. This simile* has two effects. Not only do we feel pity for the fishes (and hence for the sailors) as they gasp on the shore, but also the suggested 'whippiness' of the rod and tug of the line give us an indirect glimpse of the monster's tentacles.

3. This simile is also interesting for a more general reason. Readers of epic are familiar with the 'long-tailed' simile in which, having made his point, the poet goes on to describe a scene in greater detail than is necessary for his immediate purpose.** Here, on the other hand, we have a 'slow-starting' simile, in which the details of the fisherman's location, use of bait and float-protector do indeed bring the picture to life, but add nothing to either of the two facets of the simile which are discussed above.

4. In the second section of the narrative (ll.66–90) Homer is as careful to avoid repeating details of Charybdis as in the previous section he was to avoid repeating details of Scylla. No doubt this is because in each case he wishes his hearers to concentrate on the psychology of the situation; the device is carefully worked out and quite sophisticated. He now concentrates on the feelings of Odysseus as he hangs 'like a bat' from the roots of the strange fig-tree, whose existence was mentioned to him by Circe. Roots of trees seem to be a symbol of safety for Odysseus: cf. *Od. v.*, 475 ff., Passage V. The poet stresses once more Odysseus's amazing powers of endurance: the long hours are emphasized in the simile (ll.80–3), which may well depict, as similes in Homer often seem to, the

* Cf. Passage XIX (a) 1.7 – the same picture, but with a quite different tone, this time one of ruthlessness.
** Cf. the fine example in Matthew Arnold's *Sohrab and Rustum* of the 'cunning workman in Pekin' who 'pricks with vermilion some clear porcelain vase'.

customs of the poet's own day rather than those of the heroic age. With the phrase 'casting shadow out over Charybdis', we are given a hint of the sun's movement overhead, and the feeling of a never-ending day is as vivid for the reader as Nehemiah's description:* 'So we laboured in the work; and half of them held spears from the rising of the morning till the stars appeared'. In each case the effect is obtained with great economy of words.

5. It is clear that Homer wished to describe two hazards which could not both be undergone during one transit of the narrows. He is unwilling to omit either adventure and is therefore driven to the device of sending Odysseus back into the straits alone. This is perhaps somewhat artificial, but the artificiality would be less noticeable to an audience than it is to the eye of the reader. It is a feature of Homer's narrative technique that he is always unwilling, even at some cost to the structure of the poem,** to sacrifice an exciting episode.

Commentary

6. ll.1–7. Lines 201 and 206–7 of the Greek are completely formulaic. In between, the phrases for the most part have no known parallel in *Odyssey* or *Iliad*, and some of them are striking; e.g. in Gk. 202:

– kápnōn kái mégă kúmă ídōn kái dóupŏn ăkóusă –

('I caught sight of spray and heavy seas, and I heard a dull thudding')

the general effect is visual, but the one heavy word *doupon* ('thudding') gives us, by contrast, the noise of waves breaking against the rock, and in Gk. 204 ('the oars flew from their hands') the sound of the verb *bōmbésan* represents the clatter of oars against the thole-pins or against the side of the ship as the men stop rowing.

7. l.5 'The ship lost way.' The line (Gk. 205) begins with the monosyllable *nēus* ('ship'), after which there is a

---

* *Nehemiah* 4, 21.
** Cf. Passage XVII, Appreciation 1-2.

pause. This perhaps indicates the check as the ship loses way. It has been argued that such pauses have no significance, and statistics do show that they are not always meaningful; but anyone who reads the poem aloud must surely feel that in many places, as here, a pictorial effect was intended.*

8. l.36 'spray-clad rock'. The G4eek adjective is *éĕrŏéidĕă*, which usually means 'grey' or 'misty'. It is a standard epithet for the sea. Homer here transfers it to the cliff-wall which is hidden by clouds of spray – a good example of how a stock epithet may be 'revivified' by being transferred to a fresh context.

9. l.40 'like a cauldron on a hot fire': a simile from daily domestic life. Sometimes Homer goes further than this: cf. *Od. xx.* 24 ff., where Odysseus, deeply worried at the debased behaviour of the maid-servants in his palace, is described as follows: 'He tossed and turned, as when a man shifts a haggis full of fat and blood on a hot fire, wanting it to be cooked quickly'. One feels that such a tone, though it may be appropriate in the more homely atmosphere of the *Odyssey*, would not have been acceptable in the *Iliad*.

10. l.53. 'Calling on me by name: that was the last time'. This is a fine touch. Odysseus says that the men called on him *èxŏnŏmāklédēn* ('by name'), a huge word at the beginning of the line which seems to conjure up and dwell on the repeated cry of 'Odysseus'. He adds immediately 'that was the last time', which makes the hearer imagine a whole series of previous occasions on which a similar appeal was successful. Now at last even Odysseus can do nothing for them, and perhaps the death of these six men symbolizes the coming doom of the whole crew.

11. l.64 'the paths of the sea'. The phrase is simply a periphrasis for 'the sea'. Curiously, it is not used elsewhere in Homer, though it has a formulaic ring. It is not strictly a 'kenning' (like 'whale-road' and 'gannets' bath' in *Beowulf*) because it is not in origin pictorial. Perhaps it may be an

---

* Cf. Passage IX, Appreciation, 2.

'incipient formula', one which has not yet been firmly adopted.

12. 1.71 Virtually a repition of 1.38; the line therefore carries with it for the hearer the memory of the scene there described – a setting more reminiscent of the Atlantic than the Mediterranean.

13. 1.82–3 (Gk. 440) The rhythm of the line is noteworthy in that the word-stresses in the first half all fall on the first syllable of the foot, and the ends of the first two feet coincide with the ends of words.* Thus:

krínōn| néikĕă| póllă dĭkāzŏmĕnōn āĭzéōn|

There is also a metrical inversion of fourth and fifth feet.** The effect of all this on the hearer is that the line seems to be 'unbalanced'; it may be that we are intended to feel the fatigue of the long day's work in court.

14. 1.86 'I splashed down'. The word *éndōupésă* is from the same root as *doupon* ('thud') in 1.3. At the beginning of the episode Odysseus heard the thud of the breakers in the distance; now he himself is alone among them, struggling for his life.

---

* For technical reasons both these things are unusual. Cf. Intro. 6.
** Cf. Passage VIII, Appreciation, 2.

XII

Shipwreck

(a) Odyssey xii. 403-425, (b) Virgil, Aeneid i. 102-123*

Introduction

The Odyssey passage immediately precedes the second part of Passage XI. At *Aen. i.* 102 we see Aeneas and his flotilla at sea after sailing from Sicily. They are heading for Italy, but Juno's machinations produce a violent storm which drives them off-course in the direction of Africa.

Translations

(a) 'The island of Sicily was dropping behind, and there was no other land in sight – only sky and sea. At that moment Zeus, Kronos' son, checked a dark cloud over the hollow ship, and beneath that cloud
5 the sea misted over. The ship went running on, but not for long; soon came a hurricane, screaming and boiling with the storm inside it. A gust of wind snapped both forestays: the mast fell backwards, and all the gear spilled into the hold. The mast
10 itself caught the helmsman on the head as he stood at the stern – smashed every bone in his head. Like an acrobat he plummeted from the deck, and his noble soul left its frame. At the same time Zeus thundered, and hurled his bolt upon the ship; at the
15 shock she spun round and filled with sulphur-fumes. My companions dived overboard, and, like cormorants, bobbed in the water round the black ship; they were not destined to return home. For myself, I paced the ship till a roller stripped the keel from the
20 side-walls and separated it for the waves to carry, dashing the mast against it. The back-stay, made of ox-hide, was still attached, and with it I lashed

---

* As readers may know some Latin and the passage depends for its effect on being read aloud, it is printed in full, with scansion marks, at the end of this section.

60

23   the pair of them together; then, sitting astride, I
      was borne along by the deadly winds.'

      (b) As Aeneas cried out, a gust with the North wind
      in its teeth took the sail full centre and lifted the
      waves sky-high. Oars were snapped, the prow fell
      away, and the ship lay broadside on to the winds.
5   A jagged crest of water fell on her in a mass. One
      ship was poised on a wave-crest; for another, the
      wave-trough yawned so deep that land was visible
      below. The water seethed with sand. Three times the
      South wind seized Aeneas' ship and drove her
10   towards those hidden reefs out at sea which the
      Italians call the Altars – a huge chine of rock out in
      mid-ocean; three times the Easterly drove her back
      from the deep to the shallows of the Syrtes and – a
      grim sight it was – dashed her on the shoals and piled
15   a wall of sand round her. One ship, carrying Orontes
      and his loyal band of Lycians, was pooped before
      Aeneas' very eyes by a huge sea, and the helmsman
      was thrown overboard, somersaulting. As for the
      ship, the power of the sea spun her three times in
20   her own length, and a maelstrom swallowed her. In
      that wild water here and there men were to be seen
      swimming, and across the sea floated their gear,
      with some pictures, and the treasures of Troy, all
      swallowed by the deep. The tempest overcame
25   Ilioneus' strong ship, then brave Achates'; Abas
      went down, and old Aletes too. All the rest, their
      joints strained, gaping at the seams, took in the
      hostile spray.

Appreciation

      1. The two passages should be read side by side, and
a comparison may be made with Passage V, which however is
different in its centre of interest.

2. Homer's lines at first sight seem stark, almost over-simplified. The narrative gives detail after detail, beginning with the gathering storm, then focusing closely on the single doomed ship, whose fate becomes increasingly certain as first the helmsman is killed, then the crew go overboard and are drowned. Odysseus, however, clings to the only safety he can see clearly, until finally the ship falls apart and he must save himself by making a life-raft. Even in this crisis he remains cool, thinks for himself, and uses the best material he can lay hands on. The poet shows no pity for him, and Odysseus does not pity himself; all is factual, and in the end the hero finds himself alone, the sole survivor of his ship, and in a desperate situation. Evidently he is going to escape, but the sheer force of the poetry, with its brutal accumulation of detail, so overwhelms the reader that he has no time for any such comforting reflection; we are battered and bruised as Odysseus was, and identify ourselves fully with him.

3. The means by which this effect is obtained are noteworthy. First of all the marine technicalities are convincing; we see in detail the Homeric ship with its simple rig (two forestays, one backstay, a lateen sail), and the scene is convincingly painted as she gradually falls apart, first losing her mast and rigging, then disintegrating under Odysseus' feet as he prowls up and down. All this is reinforced by the sound of the words as the storm strikes (l.6):

áipsă găr élthĕ

kēklégŏs Zĕphŭrōs mĕgăl̄e sŭn láilăpĭ thŭ̄on
hístōu dé prŏtŏnŏus ērréx' ănĕmóiŏ thŭéllă

(Gk. 407–9)

The sounds *p*, *ph*, *t*, *th* give something of the force of the gusts, and anyone who reads the lines aloud must feel that there is a storm in progress (cf. Passage III, Appreciation, 1).

4. The two similes both illustrate the sudden departure of the crew: the helmsman, dead and catapulted overboard by a blow from the mast: the sailors who, terrified by the thunderbolt, dive overboard and then are seen only as heads which bob briefly on the water, like sea-birds.

5. In the middle of this inferno Odysseus (the unmistakable centre of the picture, by contrast with Passage V) is left alone, still calculating his best chance. We are made to feel that he is now entirely defenceless, stripped of ships, companions and divine help. If he can get out of this disaster, he deserves to survive.

6. The brevity which Homer uses in moments of tension is very effective. In l.5 the ship 'kept going, but not for long'. In l.16 the men are in the sea, but alive; there is still hope. In the next line we are told simply that 'they were not destined to return', and we neither hear nor see any more of them. The laconic grimness with which a hoped-for future is thus demolished is very impressive. We shall meet it again in Passage XIX, where it is discussed more fully.

7. The passage from the Aeneid is much more elaborate and seeks a different effect. Here we are dealing not with one ship but with a flotilla; not with the survival of a single man, but with the persistence of the spirit of Troy to be a component part of Roman history. The fate of several ships is described in detail, and although Virgil clearly had the Homeric passage in mind (e.g. in (b) ll.17–18 (=Lat. 115–16), where the helmsman is thrown overboard) he is not so much stripping Aeneas personally of his resources (Aeneas' ship, though stranded, does in the end survive, and so in fact do most of the others) as demonstrating by how narrow a margin the whole expedition came through. The crews who are lost reduce the strength of the Trojan element which will get through to Italy, and the picture of the wealth of Troy adrift on the waters symbolizes the loss of cultural and artistic traditions. The word used for 'treasure' is 'gaza', a loan-word originally descriptive of the state-treasures of the Persian empire; it is thus appropriate in a context where great power and great antiquity are symbolized. In the end Aeneas will have lost most of what he brought from Troy in the shape of

external possessions. He will have been moulded and educated by his adventures, and what he brings from Troy will be inside himself.

8. On the technical level, the writing is of a different kind from Homer's. There are certain rhetorical effects: thus in 1.3 the waves are 'sky-high', and in 1.28 the sea, as it comes between strained planks, is 'the hostile spray'. Sentences are carefully balanced (*'Three times* the South wind . . . *three times* the Easterly . . . ')' More lines are enjambed than in Homer, and the enjambment is more complete, so that in the end we have the impression of a verse-paragraph. In (b) 1.21 (=Lat. 105) the line ends *prāerŭptŭs ắq́uāe mố́nś* where the unusual monosyllable depicts the towering wave. In (b) 1.21 (=Lat. 118) the very spondaic *āppắrènt rắŕī nắnt́ēs iń ǵúrgĭtĕ vắstờ* ('In that wild water here and there men were to be seen swimming') marks a strong contrast with the turbulence which has preceded, and introduces the next and very evocative line about the 'treasures of Troy'. At every point we receive an impression of absolute technical mastery consciously deployed for the purposes which Virgil has in mind. Every word has been deliberately chosen and deliberately placed; every rhythm is there for a purpose. Some readers feel, as a consequence of all this, that Virgil is 'artificial', and it is perhaps true that his appeal is less immediate than Homer's. The picture which he gives here is a general one, and the reader's eye ranges widely over a huge canvas, on which the ships appear to be destroyed inexorably, one by one. Over this picture the poet distributes unremitting care, attending equally to every detail; the camera is at a great distance, so that we obtain a 'synoptic' view, but the lens is so good that every outline is sharp. The technique is different from Homer's, and the purpose is different, but it is impossible to deny the power of the writing.

Aen. i. 102–123. Latin Text.

Tălĭă iāctántī strídēns Ăquĭ́lónĕ prŏcéllă
Vélŭm ădvérsă fĕ́rīt, flŭ́ctūsqŭé ăd sídĕră tóllĭt.
Frāngúntūr rĕ́mī; túm prórȧ āvértĭt, ĕt úndīs
10 Dát lătŭs; ĭnsĕquĭ́tūr cŭmŭ́lō praĕrúptŭs ăquae mōns.
Hī́ súmmø iñ flŭ́ctū péndēnt; hī́s úndă dĕhī́scēns
Térrȧm íntĕr flŭ́ctūs ăpĕ́rĭt, fŭ́rĭt aéstŭs hărénīs.
Trī́s Nŏtŭs ābrĕ́ptās īn sáxă lătÉntĭă tórquĕt,
Sáxă vŏ́cānt Ĭtălī mĕdĭ́īs quae iñ flúctĭbŭs Árās,
110 Dórsŭm īmmánĕ mắrī súmmō; trís Eŭrŭs ăb áltō
Iñ brĕvĭa ĕt Sŷ́rtīs úrguēt, mĭsĕrábĭlĕ vísū,
Ĭnlidĭtquĕ vắdīs átquĕ ággĕrĕ́ cíngĭt hărénāe.
Ūnăm, quaé Lŷ́cĭōs fĭdúmquĕ vĕhébăt Ŏróntēn,
Ípsĭŭs ántĕ ŏcŭlōs íngēns ā vértĭcĕ́ póntŭs
115 Īn púppĭm fĕ́rĭt: ēxcŭtĭ́tūr prónūsquĕ mắgístĕr
Vólvĭtūr iñ căpŭt; ást íllām tér flúctŭs ĭ́bídĕm
Tórquĕt ắgēns círcŭm, ĕt răpĭ́dūs vŏ́răt aéquŏrĕ vórtĕx.
Āppárĕnt rárī nántēs īn gúrgĭtĕ vástō,
Ắrmă vĭ́rūm tắbŭlaequĕ́ ĕt Tróĭă gáză pĕr úndās.
20 Iām vălĭ́dam Ĭ́lĭŏneī nắvĕm, iắm fórtīs Ăchátī,
Ēt quắ véctŭs Ắbās, ĕt quắ grắndaévŭs Ălétēs,
Vícĭt hĭ́emps; lắxīs lătĕ́rūm cōmpágĭbŭs ómnēs
Āccĭ́pĭŭnt ĭnĭ́mícyŭm ímbrēm, rĭ́mīsquĕ fătíscūnt.

(*Note:* the syllables crossed out with an oblique line are 'elided'; that is, they
were either not heard or slurred into the following vowel.)

Magic voyage

Odyssey xiii. 70-92

Introduction

Odysseus has completed his tale in the presence of King Alcinous, and the Phaeacians, having bestowed gifts on him, honour their promise to take him back to Ithaca in one of their ships.

Translation

When the party had reached the ship in its berth, the noble escort already aboard quickly took the gifts and placed them in the hollow ship, all the food and drink. For Odysseus they laid down blan-
5 ket and linen, that he might sleep soundly on the deck of the hollow ship, at the stern. Up got Odysseus and lay down, all in silence. The crew sat in groups on the thwarts in due order, and cast off the hawser from the mooring-post. Then they swung to
10 their oars and churned up the sea. Meanwhile sweet sleep fell on Odysseus' eyelids, a marvellous sleep, almost as deep as death. The ship was running on, her stern lifting, while behind her surged the wash, a great seething roller of the thundering ocean. Her
15 movement was like that of four horses yoked to-gether in a chariot, when all gallop together across the plain as the charioteer whips them up; they almost leave the ground as they swiftly accomplish their journey. So the ship sped on, steady and safe.
20 Not even the falcon, fastest of winged creatures, could have kept up with her. She sped swiftly on her way, with a man aboard who for cunning was the equal of the gods. Till then he had suffered heart-ache for the many troubles which he bore as he
25 thrust his way through the warfare of men and the

26   terrible waters; but now he slept like a child and
     forgot all his sufferings.

Appreciation

1. The passage is one of great beauty and also of
great importance to the balance of the poem, as it provides
the link between the wanderings of Odysseus and the revenge
which he is to exact when he returns home. He has demon-
strated his heroic qualities under every kind of stress, both
in the real world of fighting and shipwreck and also in his
struggles against monsters and other supernatural creatures.
Now he is asleep, while the magical ship carries him swiftly
back to Ithaca; perhaps the ship symbolizes the world of
romance which Odysseus is leaving behind him at this point,
while the surge of the sea symbolizes his ordeals. Odysseus
himself is fast asleep, so much so that he does not wake when,
at *Od. xiii.* 119–20, the Phaeacians unload him and his gear; his
sleep has something strange about it, as if he were dead, and
would be a new man when he wakes up. Indeed, something like
this actually occurs, for when he wakes he is back in Ithaca,
on the well-known beach of his own island-home, yet he fails
to recognize it; his 'new personality' is not yet fully assembled, and it is only with the help of Athene that he comes
finally to his senses and sets about the task which lies before
him.

2. These lines provide a remarkable example of the
power of formulaic verse narrative. They are composed almost
entirely of phrases or whole lines which are used again elsewhere, and some of them may be deliberate reminiscences, as
when at 1.23 Homer says that Odysseus had 'suffered heart-
ache for the many troubles he bore'; the phrase occurs also in
the Prologue (*Od. i.* 1–4), and no doubt the poet wishes us to
observe that this is indeed that same hero whom he described
early in the poem, but who is now mature enough to tackle
further problems that lie before him. In general, however,
the effect of the formulae is to create a stylized surface, a

kind of enamel, which might seem an unlikely means for conveying the deep feeling which is in fact perceived. In a somewhat similar way, though by very different linguistic means, the polished, artificial texture of Milton's *Lycidas* manages to convey the poet's deep sense of loss at the untimely death of his friend, Edward King. How does Homer achieve his effect?

3. The first point is that a formula is not a cliché. In one sense both types of phrase are 'time-savers'; they remove the need for creative thought and allow the speaker, by using well-worn words and phrases, to transmit what he has to say with a minimum of exertion for himself and his hearers. But the cliché is a tired or second-rate brain's re-action to stimulus; the speaker simply cannot be bothered to look for a better way of expressing his thought. Moreover, the words used are seen on analysis to be weak and ineffective; they say twice what only needs to be said once ('this day and age') or they exaggerate and are ponderous where simplicity would be more effective ('an agonizing re-appraisal'). Neither of these criticisms is valid against the formula. Here the bard does not offer us something essentially second-rate, but rather what may well be the only phrase available to him for describing what he is trying to express. A rough sea, if it is to be described at the end of a line, is for Homer invariably 'thundering', and rowers invariably 'churn up the sea'. No doubt these things could be said differently, but generations of bards have found this phrase the most effective; our singer, unless he is trying out a deliberate innovation of his own, will use his formula without question, not because he is too lazy to think of something better, but because he does not believe that anything better could be devised. The result is that a formulaic style, far from being dead and ineffective as clichés always are, remains taut and alive; the galloping horses, the hawk which is 'fastest of winged creatures', the man who 'suffers heart-ache for many troubles' – all these phrases retain an undiminished intensity.

4. Secondly, the style has within itself a capacity for stirring the imagination to a surprising extent. The simile of the four stallions and the comparison with the hawk are perfectly simple and perfectly direct. Although obviously appropriate, they are not in themselves particularly striking. Yet the overall impression is of an unusually fine passage which is excellently suited to its context. This is perhaps because no other Homeric ship is so described; we may know the simile and the comparison from elsewhere, but we feel their power afresh because of their novel application. This ship is something special. All Phaeacian ships have magical powers, as King Alcinous tells us by implication at *Od. vii.* 186–206, and to the crew this seems to be just another voyage; they are not to know that for them it will end in disaster. But for Odysseus the swift overnight transition from the strange and wonderful land of the Phaeacians back to his native Ithaca is something miraculous, and the miracle is appropriately emphasized by the poet when he uses two comparisons which stand out because of their new surroundings. We may feel that this effect is emphasized by the completely standard lines describing 'departure by sea' which have been heard immediately beforehand.

5. Thirdly, we see again the 'distancing' effect which was noticed at the end of Passage I. As soon as the voyage has begun and Odysseus has fallen into his death-like sleep, the camera recedes and we see the ship from an ever-increasing distance. The chariot-simile perhaps increases our sensation of being spectators who look on at this 'symbolic' ship while it travels by night (a thing unusual in the ancient world) between Phaeacia and Ithaca at a turning-point in the story. A similar effect is obtained at the beginning of Thornton Wilder's *Woman of Andros*, where the viewpoint is so remote that we can see the whole Mediterranean: 'The earth sighed as it turned in its course; the shadow of night crept gradually along the Mediterranean, and Asia was left in darkness . . . The sea was large enough to hold a varied weather; a storm played about Sicily and its smoking mountains, but at the mouth of the Nile the water lay like a wet pavement. A fair tripping breeze ruffled the Aegean, and all the isles of Greece felt a new freshness at the close of day.'* In such a context it is not surprising to find that rare thing, a personal comment by the poet (ll.22–7); the poet too is standing back from his story, in which the narrative flow is momentarily at a stand-still, and allowing us briefly to share his own view of the hero.**

Commentary

6. In ll.10–12 the description of Odysseus' deep sleep is cumulative. It is first of all 'pleasant' (*nédŭmŏs*), the stan-dard epithet. Then a whole line is devoted to a fuller descrip-tion: it is a sleep 'without awakening' (*négrĕtŏs*), 'delightful' (*hēdístŏs*), and finally 'more like death than sleep' (*thănătō ānchístă ĕóikōs*). This accumulation of four separate qualifications is highly effective and impresses on the reader the almost mesmerized quality of Odysseus' slumber. The hero must not personally observe his transit; were all Phaeacian passengers 'put under' in this way so that they should not be able to reveal any secrets? The depth of Odysseus' sleep is in fact suggestive of a whole world of magical power through which, because of the esteem in which the Phaeacians hold him, he is transported without harm. 'Heureux qui, comme Ulysse, a fait un beau voyage'.***

7. In ll.13–17 a 'rocking-horse' effect is apparently being described. To the modern reader the picture seems curious, and in fact it is not quite easy to visualize the scene. We are accustomed to speed-boats which lift their bows when travelling fast, and Homer's picture of a huge wake also suggests pressure at the stern. A 'stern-up' attitude is clearly impossible, and one can only suppose that Homer is giving a

* Thornton Wilder, *The Woman of Andros*, p.1 (Longmans, 1930).
** Cf. the similar moment at *Od. xvii*. 201-2.
*** J. du Bellay (*Oxford Book of French Verse*, no. 78).

picture of a fast many-oared ship getting into its stride. We notice that Homer is concerned to establish the fact that, despite the speed, it is all quite safe (1.19).

8. The specific description of Odysseus as 'a man who for cunning was the equal of the gods' is likely to be an intentional emphasis. Odysseus has been among the magical Phaeacians, and has endured extreme peril by land and sea; he is indeed only a mortal man, yet there is something almost divine about him. In the Greek, the words for 'man' and 'gods' stand very near to each other, creating emphasis by their near-juxtaposition.

9. In structure, the passage is noticeably end-stopped. Only at two places does the sense run fully on into the next line. This fact is perhaps the product of the techniques described in the earlier part of this appreciation; if Homer was indeed using old formulae in a new way, it is likely that he would be compelled to work line by line, because that is the nature of formulae. It does not seem likely that any structural pattern or effect was intended.

10. In conclusion, one must add that a passage of this quality, with its almost lyrical intensity, makes translation hopeless. The original is both formal and at the same time deeply moving in a way which no prose version can hope to recapture.

The abduction of Eumaeus

Odyssey xv. 403-484

Introduction

Odysseus, back in Ithaca, has taken shelter with his faithful swineherd, Eumaeus, who does not recognize his disguised master. There is a pause in the story while we await the return of Telemachus, and at this point Eumaeus, in response to Odysseus' questioning, tells how he first came into the service of Laertes, father of Odysseus.

Translation

'There is an island called Syrie – you may have heard of it – away beyond Ortygia, at the sun's turning-point; not such a very populous place, but a good spot, with plenty of cattle and sheep, and full
5   of vines and wheat. No poverty touches the people, nor any other of the plagues that afflict mankind in its feebleness. No; when folk grow old there in the city, Apollo approaches, lord of the silver bow, and Artemis also; with his gentle weapons he visits
10 and slays them. The island contains two cities, between which all its territory is divided. My father (his name was Ktesios, son of Ormenos) ruled over both, more like an immortal than a human being.

'Syrie was visited by Phoenicians – famous sea-
15 men and famous swindlers, with a hoard of eye-catching stuff in their dark ship. Now my father kept a Phoenician nursery-maid in his house; a fine big woman she was, good at household jobs; and these crafty Phoenicians got round her. First of all,
20 when she was doing the washing, one of them seduced her beside the hollow ship, protesting his love for her – a thing which takes away the wits of the whole female sex, even those that are properly

trained. Then he asked her who she was and where
25 she came from, and she told him of the high-vaulted
palace of her father. "My birthplace (and I'm proud
of it) was Sidon, rich in bronze; I am the daughter
of Arybas, a man rich as can be. Taphian pirates
seized me as I was coming home from the fields, and
30 brought me across the seas to the halls of this man.
Oh, he gave them a fair price."

'The man who had seduced her said: "And now
would you like to get back home again with us, to
see the high vaults of your parents' hall and your
35 mother and father themselves? For they are still
alive, and are said to be well-off."

'The woman answered him and said: "And that
could be, if you sailor-men were willing to bind
yourselves with an oath to bring me back home safe
40 and sound." Well, they all swore according to her
formula, and when they had finished swearing and
had completed the oath, the woman spoke again
and took things further. "Quiet now! No one from
your company must so much as say a word to me if
45 he meets me in the street or perhaps at the spring
– or else somebody will go to the great house and
blab to the old man. He'll suspect something, put
me in irons, and think up some disaster for you.
You keep my plan in your heads, and press on with
50 the sale of your goods. When the ship gets full of
provisions, then quickly have a message sent to me
in the house; for I'll bring real gold, whatever comes
to hand – and I'd be glad to pay for my passage in
another way too. It's my master's son I look after
55 in the palace, ever such a crafty little fellow, just
old enough to run out of doors along with me. I
could bring him aboard, and he'd fetch a marvellous
price wherever you put him on sale among
foreigners."

60 'With those words she went off to the palace and its luxury. A whole year the men stayed with us there, and traded till their ship was full of goods. When she was loaded, ready for them to sail, they sent a messenger to warn the woman. It was a man

65 with his wits about him who came to my father's hall, bringing a necklace of gold interlaced with amber. In the great hall the serving-girls and my good mother handled it lovingly and feasted their eyes on it, promising the price asked. He however

70 fixed his eye on the woman and nodded – never a word. She took me by the hand and led me out of doors, away from the palace. In the porch she found some cups on the tables, used by banqueters who were attending my father. They had gone off to a

75 session of talk at the people's assembly. The woman hid three goblets in her bosom and made off with them, while I in my childish folly went with her. Down went the sun, and all the streets fell into shadow. We went fast and got down to the great

80 harbour where the swift Phoenician ship was berthed. They put us aboard, embarked themselves, and began to sail over the deep waters, Zeus sending them a breeze. For six days and nights we sailed on like that. But when Zeus, son of Kronos, brought

85 the seventh day, then Artemis, archer-goddess, struck the woman; she fell with a thud into the hold, just like a tern diving. Well, they threw the corpse overboard for seals and fishes to find; and there I was left, pretty sorry for myself. Wind and

90 water brought them to Ithaca, where Laertes drew on his stores and bought me. That's how I first set eyes on this land of Ithaca.'

Appreciation

1. Eumaeus is that familiar figure, the prince snatched from his cradle by a wicked servant and now seen

working for his living as a menial in a 'far country'. He is
evidently a character for whom Homer has a fondness, as is
clear from the fact that he alone in the Odyssey is regularly
apostrophized. Homer will not tell us how 'Eumaeus groaned
and said . . . ', but rather 'With a groan, Eumaeus swine-herd,
you answered and said'.* He is to be one of Odysseus' few
helpers in the final battle, and it is natural that the audience
should wish to know something about him. Odysseus will of
course know the story already, but it is in character for him
as a wandering beggar to prompt the swineherd to give us this
information. However, the tale occupies 81 lines at a critical
moment in the plot, and one cannot help feeling that it was a
story already available to the bard and retained here simply
because it was too good to miss. We seem therefore to be looking at a sort of 'fly in amber'. It is also possible that in a
different version of the plot Eumaeus may have been a more
important figure than he is in our Odyssey,** in which case the
biography would be more reasonable.

2. A relevant point in this connection is that
Eumaeus' homeland has no geographical location. 'Syrie' is
unknown; the only Ortygia (='quail-land'***) known in the
historical period was at Syracuse; and 'the turning-point of
the sun' might equally well mean 'far to the East' or 'far to
the West'. The lines feel as if they belong properly to the 'land
of plenty' theme which also underlies the description of the
palace of King Alcinous (cf. Passage VII). This feeling is reinforced by the description of Syrie in a single line of four
words as 'with plenty of cattle and sheep, and full of vines
and wheat':

éubŏtŏs eumélŏs oínŏpléthēs pŏlŭpúrŏs

* It is true that the vocative gives a convenient line-ending, but we need not
suppose that the bard was much influenced by this.
** Cf. W. J. Woodhouse, *The Composition of Homer's Odyssey*, pp.194-8 (cf. Bibliography).
*** The 'quail-island' mentioned at *Od. v.* 123 seems to be a different place, perhaps Rheneia, near Delos.

All four words are compound adjectives, and the combined effect is to emphasize the prosperity of the place. The absence of illness, and the gentle* coming of death to the old, lead us to feel that this place, whatever its origin, (and we must remember that Eumaeus is giving us a dimly-recollected and perhaps a romanticized picture of his distant childhood) lies somewhere not far away from paradise. The setting, which is made more specific by the 'two cities', thus makes us feel all the more that this biographical tale is indeed an interlude in the main narrative.

3. The conjecture that the passage may have an independent origin seems to be supported by stylistic considerations also. The tone throughout has a colloquial ring which is quite unusual, as if the story had once been told wholly in the vernacular. It is difficult to pin this down, as the outward appearance of the words is no less formulaic than in the rest of the poem; but one feels, particularly in the direct speech between the Phoenician traders and the nursery-maid, a sort of roughness beneath the polished exterior. Thus in 1.28 the woman says that her father was 'rich as can be', or 'ever so rich'. The phrase, which is not found elsewhere in Greek literature, sounds like a piece of dialect, as if a West-Riding girl were to say that her father was 'not without', meaning that he was very·well-off. The woman has an 'eye to the main chance'; she reports with pride that her purchasers 'gave a fair price'. A similar kind of expression is found in 1.37: 'And that could be' is a phrase which, in Greek as in English, eagerly but somewhat brusquely picks up the offer which the sailor has just dangled before her. Finally, the same tone of voice is heard in 1.55, where the woman describes the young Eumaeus as 'ever such a crafty little chap'. The whole tale seems in fact to belong to a commercial, huxtering society below the level of 'heroic' interest. The poet gives us a picture of the

---

* Apollo and Artemis are always the bringers of sudden (often painless) death: Apollo for men, Artemis for women. (cf. 1.85 and Passage XVI, Transl. 1.18)

Phoenicians which corresponds with their literary image through the centuries.

4. Yet after all the story is a moral one. The woman dies with mysterious suddenness, and her body is unceremoniously dumped. Eumaeus, the innocent victim, is sold into captivity, and may thus seem to have suffered the same fate as originally befell his betrayer, but in the end he attains a position of responsibility, shows continuing loyalty to his master, and has the satisfaction of becoming an essential ally in Odysseus' revenge. Throughout the passage, the contrast between the colloquial undertones of the dialogue and the moral lesson which is being imparted resembles that of the story of the woman of Samaria in St. John's Gospel. There too the formality of the diction masks a live conversational interchange:* 'Jesus saith unto her "Give me to drink". Then saith the woman . . . "How is it that thou, being a Jew, askest drink of me, which am a woman of Samaria? . . . Thou hast nothing to draw with, and the well is deep." ' As the story continues, the moral and spiritual lesson seems self-evident to the modern reader, but the woman remains earth-bound to the last. In spite of Jesus' reference to 'a well of water springing up into everlasting life', she pithily replies 'Sir, give me this water, that I thirst not, neither come hither to draw'. Here, as in the passage from the *Odyssey*, we feel both that the composer has a sense of humour and also that the rough words actually used have been somehow transposed into a more dignified style without losing their sting. It is extremely difficult in modern English to convey both tones at once.

---

* *St. John*, 4, 5-15 (Authorized Version).

XV

The dog called Flash[*]

Odyssey xvii. 290-327

Introduction

Telemachus has returned to Ithaca. He goes at once to Eumaeus' hut and sends the swine-herd to tell Penelope of his safe return. In Eumaeus' absence, Odysseus reveals himself. Father and son devise the outlines of a plan of action, as part of which Odysseus and Eumaeus (the latter still ignorant of his master's identity) go together to the palace.

Translation

So they kept on conversing. But there was a dog (his name was Flash); up came his head, ears pricked, as he lay there. He belonged to the much-suffering Odysseus, who had reared him but got no
5   pleasure from him, because he had to go off to the sacred city of Troy. Previously, young men had regularly set this dog against wild goats, deer and hares; but now, in his master's absence, he lay on a pile of manure and nobody cared. There was plenty
10   of it, ass-dung and ox-dung, in front of the gates, ready for Odysseus' servants to come and manure the great estate. There lay Flash, full of dog-fleas. As soon as he noticed Odysseus' approach, he wagged his tail and put back both his ears; but he had not
15   the strength to come nearer to his master. Odysseus observed him from a distance and wiped away a tear, which Eumaeus failed to see as his master questioned him. 'Eumaeus, this dog lying in the dung – he's a remarkable sight! He looks a fine
20   creature, but I can't tell for certain whether, in addition to his good looks, he used to be a good

[*] His name in Greek is 'Argos'. The translation 'Flash' is from W. B. Stanford's edition (cf. Bibliography).

courser. Perhaps he was merely one of those table-
dogs which men keep – dogs which their masters
maintain just for show.'

25   This was your answer, Eumaeus, swine-herd.
'Yes indeed, he's the dog that belongs to a man who
is dead and gone, far away. If he were at the same
peak of good looks and prowess as on the day when
Odysseus left him to go to Troy, you'd be amazed
30   to see his speed and his courage. Never would any
savage beast get away which he happened to be
pursuing in the depths of the wild wood; and he was
a splendid tracker too. But now he's lost in misery,
and his master's dead far away from his own land.
35   The women neglect him; they don't care. All servants shirk their proper jobs when the masters are
not there to control them; almighty Zeus takes
away half a chap's manhood as soon as the day of
enslavement gets him.'
40   With these words Eumaeus entered the well-set
palace and went straight for the great hall in search
of the lordly suitors. As for Flash, as soon as he had
set eyes on Odysseus after those twenty years, dark
death, his destiny, got hold of him.

Appreciation

1. This famous passage* has an appeal which perhaps
verges on the sentimental, as does the equally famous scene
between Hector and Andromache at *Iliad vi.* 390 ff. Here Homer
keeps the emotion under strict control, using various means.

2. (a) The details are exact and realistic. The pile
of manure (warm, and so comfortable): the dog-ticks: the ears
first pricked and then laid back: the dog's extreme feebleness

* Cf. the similar but much less effective scene in the story called 'The Captivity
of Dulić Ibrahim' (Parry M. and Lord A. B., *Serbo-Croatian Heroic Songs*, Vol. i,
pp. 90 ff.) where the long-absent hero returns and is recognized by his chestnut
horse.

– all these make the scene alive and credible. The very presence of a manure heap so near the palace makes us realize how reasonable it was for Telemachus to be bowled over by the glories of Menelaus' palace at Sparta;* here in Ithaca the 'palace' is more like a Saxon manor-house.

3. (b) The reaction of Odysseus is worth observing. Even from a distance he knows at once what dog this is (no-one who has trained a dog could ever forget him), and he is deeply moved. The phrase at l.16 ('he wiped away a tear') is not dwelt on; Odysseus, who cannot yet allow his identity to be known, must at all costs control himself, and he does so, 'easily escaping Eumaeus' notice'. We may remember by way of contrast how unrestrainedly he wept at the Phaeacian court, where the need for concealment was so much less pressing. To cover his feelings, he asks his host about the dog, and goes on to compliment him on its appearance. Odysseus is of course playing his part of wandering beggar; he feels it necessary to comment favourably on the appearance of even so neglected an animal as this; or perhaps he does really discern the lines of the thoroughbred whom he himself selected so long ago. At any rate he not only conceals his tears but forces himself to continue with his act of deception. A hero must not be overcome by emotion at a critical moment.**

4. (c) Homer has a grip on the realities of his tale. Flash is now twenty years old, and there is no place for him in what follows. The poet lets him die with as light a touch as when he makes Odysseus part from Nausicaa in Book *viii*.*** The sentence 'dark death, his destiny, got hold of him'–

kătă¹ móiră lăb̕en mĕlănòs thănătóiŏ –

is one of the many standard Homeric ways of describing death, and its restrained dignity is fully effective in this emotionally-charged context. There is, by contrast, some under-

---

* Cf. Passage VII, Appreciation, 1.
** Cf. *Od. xix.* 209 ff., where Penelope weeps but Odysseus again has to restrain himself.
*** Cf. Passage VI, Appreciation, 2.

lining of the pathos of the situation as the poet ends the incident by reminding us of the twenty-year lapse of time. Flash, like Eumaeus, remained faithful.

5. We have noticed that on this occasion Homer chooses to emphasize the facts about the canine life-span; he is not bound to do the same in the case of humans. Penelope and Odysseus too are twenty years older, but this fact is always glossed over in the story. We may compare Sarah's beauty at the age of ninety: see *Genesis* 17.17 and 20.2.*

Commentary

6. ll.1–3 are vivid. Odysseus and Eumaeus have been talking. In the Greek the next words are literally 'Up – a dog – his head and ears – he held them as he lay there'. The adverb early in the sentence, and the surprising new subject (we had no idea that any dog would come into this) are striking and compel the reader's attention to what follows.

7. It is possible that the word translated 'dog-fleas' in l.12 is a 'kenning'** of the type which we meet in Anglo-Saxon poetry. This is a kind of formula which is not common in Homer, and it may be that a humorous effect is intended. The word seems literally to mean 'dog-wreckers', and Homer may have meant us to smile as perhaps Hesiod also did when in his *Works and Days* he aptly described the involuted shape of an octopus by saying 'the boneless one gnaws his foot in his fireless home, his horrid pasture'.*** If humour is indeed intended by Homer, it would be quite appropriate in this earthy context of manure-heaps.

8. The tone of Eumaeus' words is matter-of-fact. He sums up Flash briskly by saying 'Yes, a fine dog once: good courser, good fighter: good tracker too'. There is some characterization here; Eumaeus is being polite to his guest, and his politeness ends, as often happens in such cases, with a piece of sententiousness (in character but irrelevant to conversation)

* Cf. Passage XVI, Appreciation, 3.
** Cf. Passage XI, Appreciation, 11.
*** Hesiod, *Works and Days*, 524–5.

about the evils of slavery. This should be read in conjunction with *Od. xi.* 488 ff., where the ghost of Achilles reflects that it is better to be even a slave on earth than to have kingly status among the dead.

9. The whole passage well illustrates Homer's habit of depicting an emotionally 'strong' situation in terms which are neutral. The reader is emotionally involved because any feeling person must have sympathy for such characters in such circumstances. Homer, underplaying the situation, releases successive waves of feeling by phrases which, precisely because they are themselves colourless, seem like doors opening to allow the emotion to develop gradually. This passage is one of the many stages of the recognition of Odysseus, and it must not be overdone, or Eumaeus too will recognize his master, and the plot does not yet permit this. No doubt the theme 'recognition by aged dog' was well known to all bards; the modern reader will perhaps feel that here it has been pared down to its bare essentials. In just the same way the reader who examines the famous scene in *Iliad xxiv*, where Priam appeals to Achilles for the body of Hector, will find that a sequence of strong emotions is 'triggered'* by words which in themselves do not speak very loudly, but which, in the context so carefully prepared, are overpoweringly effective.

* Cf. Intro. 12.

XVI

The beauty of Penelope

Odyssey xviii. 187-213

Introduction

Odysseus, still disguised, is now inside his own palace among the suitors, whom he surprises by defeating in fair fight an impressive but flabby beggar called Iros. Penelope knows only that an unidentified stranger has arrived, and she has arranged to talk with him this very evening.

Translation

Now the grey-eyed goddess Athene thought of a further plan. She poured sweet slumber over Penelope, daughter of Ikarios, so that she lay back there on her couch and slept, with all her joints relaxed.
5 Meanwhile that potent ˙goddess was giving her heavenly gifts, so that the Achaeans might admire her. First Athene cleansed the lovely face with a celestial ointment such as Aphrodite, gloriously crowned, uses to anoint herself when she goes to
10 join the fair chorus of the Graces. Also Athene made her taller and grander to look upon, whiter than fresh-cut ivory. This the potent goddess did, and so departed. White-armed maid-servants came chattering up from the great hall, so that sweet sleep left
15 Penelope, who brushed her cheeks with her hands and said 'What a gentle slumber enveloped me and my unhappiness! Would that holy Artemis would send me as gentle a death, even at this very moment, so that I might no longer waste away my life in
20 heart-felt lamentation, yearning for my dear husband and his versatile good qualities; he was indeed outstanding among the Achaeans.'

With these words she went down through the polished upper rooms – not alone, but accompanied

25   by two maid-servants. When that queen among
women reached the suitors, she stood beside a pillar
of the well-wrought roof, holding her bright veil
before her face, with a trusted handmaid on either
side. The suitors' knees turned to water; they were
30   in the grip of passionate desire, and all felt the urge
to enjoy her in bed.

Appreciation

      1. Athene plans to enhance Penelope's beauty so
that she may excite the passions of the suitors and so induce
them to bring generous gifts as a 'bride-price': gifts which will
accrue to Odysseus, who has throughout his wanderings
shown himself more than ready to enrich himself in any way
possible. (Cf. his solicitude at the beginning of *Od. xiii.* over
the gifts presented to him by the Phaeacians). Athene approves
of and encourages his acquisitiveness, and in this passage she
makes Penelope her unconscious agent, 'using' her as Aphrodite uses Helen at *Iliad iii.* 383 ff.

      2. The lines are not at first sight particularly attrac-
tive or striking, and the charms of Penelope may seem to be
inadequately represented. All that Homer actually says by
way of a description of her beauty is that Athene made her
'taller and grander'* (1.11), and that her skin became 'whiter
than fresh-cut ivory' – whiteness of skin being esteemed as
an essential part of refined female beauty in a climate where
it is rare, because difficult to maintain. Penelope herself is
only conscious of the pleasantness of the sleep which has just
left her, feeling that she has been 'lost in it', as Athene intended (cf. 1.2, 'she poured sweet slumber over Penelope'); she
knows nothing of the change in her appearance until she
observes the suitors' reaction. No motive is ascribed to her for

_____

* The actual word is 'thicker'; clearly the whole picture is of a figure 'larger
than life', perhaps almost like a goddess. Sheer size is regarded as an impressive
female trait by the Norse saga writers also. Cf. *Njal's Saga*, §9. (Penguin Classics
ed.): 'Hallgerd had grown up to be a woman of great beauty. She was very
tall . . . '

going down to the hall; as all her thoughts are on Odysseus, it would seem that Homer is telling us that her reasons were sub-conscious; he cannot describe such a psychological state except by saying that the goddess induced her to do it.

3. Nevertheless, even if Penelope is unconscious of her own beauty, the reader or listener is made very much aware of it. He may perhaps feel a certain difficulty because he knows that Odysseus has been away from home for twenty years* and that Penelope has a grown-up son. This point is irrelevant. Homer is concentrating on the immediate moment. He wishes to make Penelope beautiful, partly in order that she may be Athene's tool, partly because the woman for whom Odysseus has sacrificed so much must be presented as in all respects worthy of his efforts. It is a characteristic of early epic that when immediate considerations of this sort arise, the poet is not concerned with the past and future but only with the immediate present. Many of the supposed 'contradictions' in Homer are probably to be explained in this way. The poet, and with him the audience, is committed only to the words being uttered here and now.** It is necessary for Penelope to be beautiful, and the poet exercises his right to make her so.

4. The techniques by which the beauty is suggested are worth examining. In the first place, the poet gives it the highest superlative in his vocabulary by saying not only that it is divinely sent but also that the means used to produce it are those used by the most beautiful of the immortals on a ceremonial occasion. The Olympians are not for Homer the pasteboard figures which they become in later epic; his description is laconically expressed but extremely striking.

5. Secondly, the tranquil and elegant surface-texture of ll.1–2 is completely shattered by the ugliness of ll.29–31 with their objective description of sexuality ('they

* Cf. Passage XV, Appreciation, 5 for further comment on this point.
** Cf. my forthcoming article, 'The change of plan in the "Doloneia",' to be published in *Greece and Rome*, Oct. 1971.

felt the urge to enjoy her in bed')*. The contrast between the modesty of Penelope, proceeding with veil and customary attendance towards the hall, and the purely masculine reaction of the suitors, could not be greater. We do not learn much about Penelope's character in this incident, because she is a mere agent for the goddess, but we learn a good deal about the suitors.

6. In both these ways Homer conveys an oblique but forceful view of Penelope's charms. This is a technique familiar to readers of *Iliad iii.* 156–160, where Helen is seen on the walls of Troy, and the old men comment: 'It is no shame for Trojans and well-greaved Achaeans to suffer troubles so long for such a woman. In appearance she is terribly like the immortal goddesses. But even so, beautiful as she is, let her depart in the ships ...'. Here too, without specific or' itemizing' description, the poet creates an effect of overwhelming beauty, and we notice that the same comparison with divine beauty is employed, though in more general terms than in our passage.

7. Homer's method is the exact opposite of that used in the thirteenth century Provençal tale *Aucassin and Nicolette.* There Nicolette is described: 'She had fair hair with little curls, and her eyes blue-grey and laughing, and her face well-featured, and her nose high and well-set, and her lips redder than cherry or rose in summertide, and her teeth white and little; and her breasts were hard, lifting her robe as if they had been two walnuts; and so slim was she from flank to flank that you might have clasped her within your two hands; and the daisy-flowers broken by her toes, as they fell across the arch of her foot, were right black against her feet and legs – so white was the maid'.** Here every detail is included, and the picture is certainly sharp, though the style is degenerating

---

* Cf. the similar (but less effective) presentation of the same theme at *Od. i.* 328-366, where the poet is evidently more interested in Telemachus than in Penelope.

** Quoted by F. L. Lucas, *Decline and Fall of the Romantic Ideal,* p. 79 (Cambridge, 1936: reprinted).

into a mannered rhetoric, as the last sentence clearly shows.*
By contrast we see something very like Homer's restraint,
which is characteristic of early saga, in the story of David and
Bath-sheba in II Samuel 11: 'And David rose from off his bed
and walked upon the roof of the king's house; and from the
roof he saw a woman washing herself, and the woman was very
beautiful to look upon.' This description is reticent in the
extreme, but just enough detail is supplied to stimulate the
reader's imagination and to give motivation for the major
crime which follows. This is how Homer might have handled
the incident, and in fact it would not be hard to compose
Homeric lines to describe it.

* Cf. the similar conceit in Theocritus, *Idyll x*. 36: 'lovely Bombuka, your feet
twinkle like dice'.

XVII

The scar of Odysseus

Odyssey xix. 386-394 and 467-490

Introduction

The interview between Penelope and Odysseus (see Passage XVI, Intro.) is in progress. Odysseus is still unrecognized; he pretends that he is a Cretan who has seen Odysseus on his travels. Penelope offers a bed and hospitality, but Odysseus says that he prefers to go on 'sleeping rough', and rejects the suggestion of foot-washing 'unless there is an old woman in the house, a sensible body, who has suffered as much as I have. I should not mind if she were to wash my feet' (*Od. xix.* 346–8). At this Penelope tells the old nurse, Eurycleia, to bring washing materials, and there is some conversation between her and Odysseus.

Translation

He ended his words, and the old woman took the gleaming cauldron which she used for washing feet. She poured in plenty of cold water, and added the hot. Now Odysseus, who was sitting by the
5   fireside, quickly turned towards the shadows; he felt anxiety in his heart that as she took hold of him she would feel his scar, and everything would become known. Eurycleia came close and began to wash him – her lord. Instantly she recognized the
10   scar, which long ago a boar had gouged with its white tusk, when Odysseus had gone to Parnassus to visit Autolycus and his sons . . .
* *
This scar Eurycleia now held in the palms of her hands. As she handled it, she recognized it at once,
15   and let the foot fall free. Odysseus' shin fell into the cauldron; there was a clatter of bronze, the vessel tipped over backwards, and water was spilled all over the floor. Eurycleia's heart filled with a mix-

ture of joy and pain, her eyes brimmed with tears,
20   her voice faltered and broke. She took Odysseus by
the chin and said: 'My son, you're Odysseus, I know
for sure. To think that I didn't recognize you before
– not until I handled my lord all over'. With these
words she glanced towards Penelope, wanting to
25   tell her that her long-lost husband was home. But
Penelope could not look in her direction or even
notice anything, because Athene had diverted her
attention. Odysseus took Eurycleia by the throat
in the grasp of his right hand, while with his left he
30   dragged her nearer to him and said: 'Nanny, why
do you want to destroy me? It was you who held me
to your breast and fed me. And now, after all my
pain and trouble, I am back in my own place, with
twenty years gone. Yes, you've recognized me; and
35   a god put the idea into your mind. But now – quiet!
No one else in the great hall must discover me.
Otherwise – I tell you this and it shall be done without fail – if god by my agency destroys these lord-
lings of suitors, then, at the moment when I come
40   to execute the other serving-women in my halls, I
will not keep my hands off you, nurse of mine
though you are.'

Appreciation

1. The interest of the passage lies not so much in the
language as in two major points of narrative technique.
a) Odysseus has himself made it extremely likely (cf. Passage
XVII, Intro.) that Eurycleia will be chosen to wash his feet.
Why does he suggest the one person who, apart from Penelope
herself, is most likely to recognize the scar, when, as is clear
from the text, he does not in fact wish to make himself known
to anyone in the room?

2. The answer would seem to be, as W. J. Woodhouse*

---

* *The Composition of Homer's Odyssey*, ch. IX (cf. Bibliography).

has pointed out, that this is one of the occasions where Homer has before him a number of variants from which he can choose. The saga material evidently* offered more than one means by which a long-absent master could be recognized on his return. One such theme was 'recognition by scar', and in that version we may presume that it was always the old nurse, who, knowing her master's physical marks better than the wife, performed the recognition. The actual moment of recognition is vividly described in our passage: Eurycleia, who has previously remarked on the stranger's general physical resemblance to her master (*Od. xix*. 380–1) feels the scar with her hands (a good detail, in that, owing to Odysseus' 'avoiding action', she cannot actually see the mark of the wound), instantly feels that her earlier premonition was justified, and causes the upset described at ll.15–18. Penelope is sitting close to them, and in real life would inevitably have noticed this disturbance. Homer, however, does not yet desire a recognition between husband and wife, and consequently he must devise some plausible means of avoiding it. As soon as we consider the scene in this way, it becomes plain that Penelope's 'inattention' at ll.26–8 is in fact the poet's way of getting over the difficulty. 'Athene diverted her attention'** – because for Homer, who wishes both to retain 'recognition by scar' and yet to defer the recognition between husband and wife, a fiction of this kind, however transparent it may be when closely examined, is the only way of getting over the difficulty. (The only alternative solution, that the foot-washing should be done by Eurycleia away from Penelope's presence, would involve even greater difficulties, because the interview between Odysseus and Penelope is to continue immediately afterwards). It is particularly interesting that Homer retains the incident of the noise and the spilt water; the vivid detail

* Cf. Passage XV, Commentary, 9.
** For another instance of the same kind of thing, cf. Passage XVI, Appreciation, 2.

is too good to lose, even though it must make Penelope's 'inattention' still more unlikely. The oral poet, always look-ing for an effect which will captivate his audience, can afford a degree of unrealism – even, sometimes, of absolute incon-sistency – which would be quite impossible for a novelist.

3. (b) Between ll.12 and 13 the poem contains 70 lines (omitted in the translation) in which Homer describes how the scar was inflicted. Odysseus as a young man had gone to visit his grandfather and grandmother, Autolycus and Amphithee. A boar-hunt was held, during which Odysseus acquitted himself well but was severely gored. Eurycleia figures incidentally in this narrative also, for we are told that it was she who, many years earlier still, first put the infant Odysseus on his grandfather's knee and asked Autolycus to suggest a name for the baby. (*Od. xix.* 399–412). The story of the boar-hunt itself is given at length, with circumstantial details, and at the end of the narrative we find an example of 'ring-composition'; Homer repeats at *Od. xix.* 465–6, the sen-tence which ends in our text at l.12, so that we find ourselves back again in Odysseus' palace with Eurycleia holding his leg and recognizing the scar.

4. The modern reader's first thought will be that Homer, by interposing these 70 lines, is deliberately holding up the recognition and keeping his hearers in suspense. This may be part of the truth, but it is more likely, as Erich Auer-bach has pointed out in a famous essay,* that we are dealing with a more fundamental feature of the poet's style. It is usual for him to keep his audience fully informed of the minutest details of the scene which he is describing; everything is either sharply in focus** (cf. Passage II, Appreciation, 2) or else is omitted altogether. The technical effect is that of a painting by one of the early pre-Raphaelite school, although of course the underlying feeling is quite different. A picture such as

* *Mimesis*, ch. 1 (Princeton University Press, 1953).
** It may be this fondness for surface detail which produces the 'long-tailed simile'. (Cf. Passage XI., Appreciation, 3).

Ford Madox Browne's 'Work'* illustrates the point. There we see men digging up a pavement, rich and poor passers-by, notices on the wall, bill-board men in the distance; and so far as the eye can reach, everything is evenly illuminated and the tiniest details are clear. So it is with the story of the boar-hunt. The scar is important for Eurycleia's recognition of Odysseus, and naturally the audience will want to know how it was inflicted. The bard himself has this knowledge, and neither he nor they will be happy until the parenthetic tale is complete. At that point, to mark the closing bracket, the ring-composition motif brings us firmly back to the starting-point.

5. As within the 'digression' (though this is not how Homer would have regarded it) everything is sharp, so behind the digression lie the equally clear details of a smaller excursion into a still remoter past, the occasion when Eurycleia asked Autolycus to name the baby. The bard even has time for the words actually used. The method is leisurely, and the result is a gain in 'actuality'; the hearer feels an apparently infinite recession behind the main fabric of the story, and this helps him to believe in the reality of what is sung. The bard, it appears, knows everything** about Odysseus and his family history, just as Professor Tolkien knows everything about hobbits and can fill a large appendix with imaginary 'sources' for 'The Fellowship of the Ring'.

6. Auerbach goes on to point out the difference between such a technique and that adopted by the author of the story of Abraham's attempted sacrifice of Isaac.*** The relevant verses are worth quoting:

'And Abraham rose up early in the morning, and saddled his ass, and took two of his young men with him, and Isaac his son, and clave the wood for the burnt offering, and rose up,

---

* City Museum and Art Gallery, Birmingham.
** For another example, cf. Passage XVIII, Intro. and footnote.
*** *Genesis* 22, 3-8 (Authorized Version).

and went unto the place of which God had told him. Then on
the third day Abraham lifted up his eyes, and saw the place
afar off. And Abraham said unto his young men, "Abide ye
here with the ass; and I and the lad will go yonder, and wor-
ship, and come again to you". And Abraham took the wood of
the burnt offering, and laid it upon Isaac his son; and he took
the fire in his hand, and a knife; and they went both of them
together. And Isaac spoke unto Abraham his father and said
"My father": and he said, "Here am I, my son!" And he said,
"Behold the fire and the wood: but where is the lamb for a
burnt offering?" And Abraham said, "My son, God will provide
himself a lamb for burnt offering". So they went both of them
together.'

This is brilliantly told and extremely moving, but the
technique is very far from Homer's. There is remarkably little
surface detail: what sort of a place was it? We do not know.
Abraham obeys God's command, but neither word nor thought
is imputed to him; he simply does as he is told. Nor is there
any characterization beyond the very briefest outline, so that
the story depends for its effect on the gradual but apparently
inevitable progression of events until the final tragedy is
averted by divine intervention.

7. There is no contradiction here with what was
said at the end of the Appreciation to Passage XVI. Homer
does indeed use on many occasions the technique of understatement, but he does so after he has prepared the ground
by giving us full details of the people concerned, as in the case
of Priam and Achilles. The relationship between Abraham
and his son is nowhere so treated: they remain skeletons who
are never clothed with flesh and blood, whose story moves us
not because we know them as people but because we admire
the moral lesson which they exemplify. The Old Testament
writers simplify habitually, Homer only when he chooses to
do so. His normal way is to give us all the realistic detail we
can desire. Thus at 11.28–30 we have an exact picture of the
forcible measures taken by Odysseus to prevent Eurycleia

from speaking. His right hand has her by the throat, while his left pulls her near enough for a whisper to suffice.

Commentary

8. ll.30 ff. There is a fine contrast between the endearments with which Odysseus begins, including a reference to Eurycleia's suckling of him as a baby, and the savagery of the words which follow. The force of 'I tell you this and it shall be done without fail' is such that we believe Odysseus capable of executing the threat. If we are right in thinking that in an earlier version of the tale this recognition by the nurse was definitive, then the words of ll.30 ff, which would not in that case be necessary, must have been 'invented' by the poet who harmonized the two stories; and that may well have been Homer himself.

9. l.40 Notice that Odysseus has already made up his mind what to do withe the treacherous maid-servants. The verb of 'when I come to execute' is in the first person singular, so that when in the end Telemachus orders the killing (cf. Passage XIX), he is only putting into practice a fully-formed intention of his father's. Homer perhaps wishes, even in such a small detail as this, to emphasize the fundamental harmony between father and son. We may compare the immediate *rapport* between the two in Passage XVIII, when Odysseus nods to Telemachus: no words are necessary.

Stringing the bow

Odyssey xxi. 404-434 and xxii. 1-7
(Translated as one continuous passage)

Introduction

Penelope has proposed a contest to determine who shall wed her; if any of the suitors can string the great bow which Iphitos once gave to Odysseus,* and can shoot through 'twelve axes in a row', he shall have her hand in marriage. The suitors fail in turn even to string the bow, as does Telemachus, though the latter comes very near to success. Odysseus asks if he may try his hand; the suitors object, but are over-ruled by Penelope and Telemachus. At *Od. xxi.* 379 Telemachus puts the bow into his father's hands. Then the doors of hall and courtyard are both shut, while the suitors make contemptuous remarks about Odysseus.

Translation

So the suitors mocked him; but Odysseus, that skilled contriver, lifted the great bow and looked it over. It was like the moment when a man skilled in the lyre and its songs confidently stretches a
5 new string round its peg, fixing the twisted gut at both ends. Like that, effortlessly, Odysseus strung the great bow. With his right hand he plucked it and tested the bow-string. The string sang out beautifully, clear as a swallow's voice. The suitors
10 were much abashed, and all turned pale. There was a great thunder-clap as Zeus sent his sign, and at that the long-suffering noble Odysseus rejoiced, because the son of Kronos the wily had sent him a portent. He picked up a quick arrow which was
15 lying beside him on the table. The arrow was

---

* The story of the gift is set out in full at *Od. xxi.* 15-41. Cf. Passage XVII, Appreciation, 3.

solitary – the others lay inside the quiver, as the
suitors were soon to know to their cost. Odysseus
set the arrow against the hand-grip and plucked
string and nock together; all this as he sat there on
20 the stool. He looked in front of him and took aim,
then shot. Not one of all the axes' haft-holes did he
miss; the arrow hurtled on, out and away, heavy
with bronze. Then Odysseus spoke to Telemachus:
'Telemachus, your guest does you no discredit in
25 your hall. Seated, I have not missed the target; nor
was I long in stringing the bow. My powers are still
unabated, and the suitors were mistaken in dis-
honouring me with their abuse. Now is the moment
to go on and prepare a feast for the Achaeans – a
30 feast in the daylight. Afterwards we will sport with
them in other ways too. There will be singing,
dancing and lyre-playing; for such things should
accompany banquets.'

Those were his words, and there was a nod too,
35 and a sign with the eyebrows. Telemachus put on
his sharp sword – Telemachus, true son of Odysseus
of divine descent. He grasped his spear and stood by
the throne. He was shoulder to shoulder with
Odysseus, and fully equipped now in his gleaming
40 bronze.

At this moment Odysseus, skilled contriver,
stripped off his rags and leapt onto the great threshold. He had his bow, and the quiver full of arrows;
the quick arrows he scattered there before his feet
45 and sent a word amongst the suitors: 'This contest,
this decisive contest, is over. Now I will discover
whether I am to reach another target, one which
man never attained yet; let us see whether Apollo
will grant my prayer.'

Appreciation

1. Before we can consider this superb passage as literature, there are two technical points to be got out of the way. (a) in 1.5 the accepted text would give the meaning 'As a bard . . . easily sets a string on a new peg'. This gives a kind of sense, but surely it is strings which break, not pegs; and certainly in the case of the bow it is the string which we are interested in. A small alteration in the termination of the word for 'new' gives the version adopted here.

2. (b) An immense amount has been written about the exact nature of the competition. Did Odysseus shoot through axe-heads or axe-handles, and how were they set up? The fact is that we do not know, and for the ordinary reader the question is of little interest. Heads or handles, they were arranged in a row down the middle of the hall, and it was a very difficult task to shoot an arrow through all of them in succession. To do so from a sitting position was evidently the mark of a superlative bowman. That is all we need to know.

3. The narrative is full of significant points. Odysseus handles the bow (it is his favourite weapon, and this one is the best in his own armoury) and looks it over to make sure that all is well as he prepares to string it. Conscious of his own powers, he knows that he will not fail. This is the moment which he has waited for. He is in his own home; at last he has a weapon in his hands, and Telemachus is near. The stringing is easy – as easy as it would be for Homer to string his lyre: child's play for a skilled man, it has none the less defeated everyone else in the room, including Telemachus, whose near-success shows him to be his father's son, but not yet his equal in prowess. Odysseus tests the string; it is tight and true, and the characteristic note, 'like a swallow's call',* is heard. This brief but vivid comparison whereby the well-known sound, with its deadly import, is heard in the silence, is most effective. The suitors do not yet appreciate the whole truth, but

---

* It is probably the pitch which is referred to.

they do grasp the fact that something is seriously wrong and that it is no beggar who is among them. The omen confirms their fears and Odysseus' confidence. Everything is ready, and Odysseus puts out his hand for the single arrow, seen for a moment in close-up; it is a fatal arrow, and the first of many to come. The shot is successful, and the arrow whistles off 'out and away'. Odysseus' words to Telemachus are of double meaning, for the feast will be a feast of blood, at which the 'singing' will be men's groans. The phrase 'my powers are unabated' announces to the world what Odysseus has long known in his own heart; he is the same hero as he was twenty years ago, and against all odds he will win through.

    4. In 1.20 Odysseus is sitting on a 'footstool'. In 1.38 Telemachus stands by 'the throne'. The Greek words are unambiguous, and their choice is presumably intentional. In 1.39 Odysseus is about to reveal his identity, and it is as king that he demands allegiance. The shedding of the rags is also symbolic; the true nature of the supposed beggar becomes plainer every moment.

    5. In this vivid scene, the last touch is perhaps the best of all. The arrows are clearly seen as they lie at Odysseus' feet, waiting to be picked up. One arrow, one life – if Apollo gives his blessing. At this critical moment Odysseus remembers, as he has done many times in the story,* that even when everything seems favourable, the gods may withhold their favour and ruin all. His words are indeed an 'arrow-prayer'.

Commentary

    6. 1.5 'twisted gut'. The adjective is a 'stock epithet', but it is particularly appropriate here; Odysseus has no spare bow-string, and everything now depends on this one piece of gut. Similarly in ll.14 and 44 the arrows are 'quick'; the epithet is standard, but particularly appropriate. The suitors are for the moment defenceless, and these quick arrows will bring a

* Cf. Passage V, Appreciation, 3.

quick end. The force and brilliance of the passage as a whole ensure that we shall be ready to attend to all these details. The epithets are far from 'inert'.

7. 1.16 The single arrow is a 'loner'. The adjective in the Greek (*gúmnŏs*) stands by itself at the beginning of a line. It scans as a spondee (— —), and there is a stop immediately afterwards. In this way Homer calls attention to the word and gives it maximum emphasis.

8. ll.21–2 Two successive half-lines contain many dactyls (– ∪∪), and the sentence ends with the adjective 'bronze-heavy':

diă d' | ắmpĕrĕs élthĕ th | ŭrázē
iŏs | chălkŏbắrēs.

('The arrow hurtled on, out and away, heavy with bronze')

We are perhaps intended to visualize the effortless flight of the arrow, and also its menace; bronze is the killer-metal of the heroic age.

9. 1.34–5 'He nodded over his eyebrows': perhaps a characteristic gesture (cf. *Od. ix.* 468. and *xii.* 194). For the harmony here between father and son, cf. Passage XVII, Commentary, 9.

XIX

Vengeance

(a) Odyssey xxii. 381-389

Introduction

Odysseus, Telemachus, and a few loyal retainers
have disposed of the whole group of the suitors; only Phemius
the bard and Medon the herald are spared, on the ground that
they were forced to give their services.

Translation

Odysseus glared round his hall, in search of any
man still skulking alive and avoiding his dark
doom. He saw them all there, no small number,
sprawled in the blood and dirt; they were like fish
5 which fishermen have dragged in a meshed net up
from the grey sea onto a low-lying beach; they lie
scattered all over the sand, panting for deep water,
but the scorching sun takes their life away. Just so
the bodies of the suitors lay tumbled, one on top
10 of another.

(b) Odyssey xxii. 446-473

Introduction

Odysseus has questioned Eurycleia about the
serving-women and has told her to assemble those who have
disgraced the house by sleeping with the suitors.

Translation

So he spoke, and the women all gathered in a group,
wailing and lamenting with floods of tears. First
they began bringing out the corpses of the dead
suitors and set them down under the portico of the
5 courtyard with its strong walls, jostling one
another as they did so. Odysseus himself stood over

100

them and directed them, and they kept bringing
the bodies – they had no choice. Next they began to
cleanse the fine seats and tables with absorbent
10   sponges. Telemachus, with Philoetios and Eumaeus,
kept scraping the floor of the well-made hall with
shovels. Meanwhile the women went on carrying
the scrapings and putting them out of doors. When
they had cleansed the whole place, they brought
15   the serving-girls out of the high hall and herded
them in a pen (there was no escape) between the
round-house and the wall of the noble courtyard.
Telemachus, shrewd youngster, began to speak.
'Never may I despatch such women by honourable
20   execution – women who have poured shame on my
head and on my mother by sleeping with the
suitors.'

Those were his words. He took up a sea-going
ship's cable and knotted it round the great pillar
25   of the round-house, stretching it high up, so that
no foot would touch the ground. Sometimes long-
winged thrushes or doves stick fast in a trap set in
a thicket, as they fly home to roost; bitter is that
bed for them. So then the women had their heads in
30   a row, and there was a noose round every neck for
the nastiest of deaths. Their feet twitched a little,
but not for long.

Appreciation

1. The suitors are dead; heroic deeds have been
performed, and now Odysseus has to deal with the aftermath.
There are corpses to be disposed of, and there is the problem
of disloyal servants. Homer's mood at this point is as grim
and as factual as that of the Icelandic saga-writers, with
whom on such occasions he has, as we shall see, a good deal
in common. No concessions are made to sentiment, and no
attempt is made to gloss over unpleasant details. We see the

bodies of the suitors piled up like those of fish dying on the shore,* with the implication that the one scene is as natural as the other. Fishes are caught and killed because men must eat; usurpers are butchered because the master has come home and vengeance is necessary. There is no need for sympathy with the victims in either case. The serving-women too must be dealt with, because their behaviour has been a stain on the honour of the house, which must be cleansed both literally and metaphorically. However, they may as well be put to work first. It is not immediately clear from the narrative here that they are going to be executed, though we may well suspect this conclusion after Odysseus' words to Eurycleia at the end of Passage XVII. With less evidence, the women suspect it too, as their lamentations in 1.(b)2 show, but they hope that willing service now may redeem past treachery; hence their eagerness to impress Odysseus as he stands over them, a menacing but (so far) neutral figure. The cleansing of the great hall is described in every-day terms which by their understatement emphasize the fact that it is men's remains which are being scraped off the floor and carried away. After this task has been completed, the women are brought together in the courtyard; the words 'they herded them in a pen; there was no escape' increase the feeling that the woman have nothing to hope for. Interestingly, it is Telemachus, not Odysseus, who pronounces sentence on them. The *rapport*** between father and son is such that Telemachus knows his father's determination to execute the criminals, but it is he who has seen their behaviour over the years; he is adult now, and it is he who will perform the execution. It is Telemachus, responsible in his father's absence for the credit of the house, who has been shamed by the women's deeds, and it is he who must exact the penalty.

2. The execution is unpleasant but vividly presented. It is not quite clear how things were arranged in detail.

* Cf. Passage XI, Appreciation, 2.
** Cf. Passage XVII, Appreciation, 9.

The poet had the scene plain in his imagination, but we, who do not know what the 'round-house' was or where it stood in the courtyard, must take the technical points on trust.* Homer wishes above all to leave us with the final picture of the women hanging in a row, like a skein of vermin. In ll.31–2 is a touch of genius. The clause 'their feet twitched a little' means literally 'they panted with their feet'. It is not a new coinage for this passage, but one which Homer uses elsewhere (e.g. at *Od. xix.* 231) to describe the final convulsions of a dying animal; the sentence thus makes its effect by combining a vivid formulaic phrase with a grimly objective realism ('a little while, not so very long') which recalls such a passage as in Laxdale Saga** describes the death of the hero Bolli, who has been trapped and severely wounded by overpowering numbers:

'Bolli fell back against the wall. And now the rest of them, Halldor and his brothers, came rushing into the shieling . . . Bolli said, "It's safe now for you brothers to come a little closer than you have so far". And he said he did not think his defence would last very long now. It was Thorgerd who answered him, and said there was no need to shrink from dealing with Bolli thoroughly; she told them to finish off their work. Bolli was still standing up against the wall of the shieling, clutching his tunic tightly to stop his entrails falling out. Steinthor Olafsson now sprang at him and swung a great axe at his neck just above the shoulders, and the head flew off at once . . . With that they left the shieling. Gudrun now came walking up from the stream and went over to talk to Halldor and the others. She asked them how their encounter with Bolli had gone. They told her what had happened. Gudrun was wearing a tunic with a tight-fitting woven bodice, and a tall head-dress, and round her waist she had tied a fringed sash with dark blue stripes. Helgi Hardbeinsson went up to her and

* Detailed discussion: W. B. Stanford, Commentary on *Od. xxii.* 442. and Appendix B. (cf. Bibliography).
** *Laxdaela Saga*, tr. Magnusson and Palsson, pp. 187–8 (Penguin Books, 1969).

103

took one end of the sash and wiped the blood off the spear with which he had run Bolli through. Gudrun looked at him and smiled.'

In this passage, which might have been composed by Homer in the mood of *Odyssey xxii.*, one notices objective details such as 'to stop his entrails falling out' and 'his head flew off'; also the contrast between the masculine world of sudden, violent death and the detailed description of Gudrun's dress and appearance, leading up to the vindictive smile at her husband's death. Everything is closely observed and factually stated. We do not feel that a moral lesson is being imparted, yet the poet has taken up a certain moral position which is implicit in the narrative without being forced on the reader.

3. In Passage XIX (b) we find seven lines which, although they appear stylistically quite normal, contain almost nothing which is certifiably formulaic. It seems therefore that this particular execution-scene may well be Homer's own invention – a suggestion which receives support from its evident vividness and power.

4. It may be that, by the use of similes such as that of the dying fish and the trapped birds, Homer was seeking to hold the background of daily life firmly before his hearers.* The normality of fishing and bird-catching** is a corrective to the unpleasantness of the killings. This happens in the Icelandic sagas also, so that Magnusson and Palsson can say,*** 'The saga . . . 'paints a vivid and unforgettable picture of living society . . . No one exists without a relation to this society; men die making charcoal, or trading, or carting dried fish, or herding live-stock'. Homer does not describe his heroes as dying in such contexts, because they live in an aristocratic

---

* Cf. also Passage I, Appreciation, 3.
** There is no pictorialism in the adjective 'long-winged' (1.27), as there was in Passage II (a). Here the word is neutral, as the context shows, being hardly more than a space-filler.
*** *Njal's Saga*, tr. Magnusson and Palsson, Intro, pp. 17-18 (Penguin Books, 1960).

age, but he himself is very familiar with such settings, and by means of his similes he makes us constantly aware of them.

XX

The Ithaca theme

(a) *Odyssey iv. 601-608*

Translations

'The horses I will not take to Ithaca; I will leave
them here for your own pleasure. You, Menelaus, are master
of a broad plain, in which is plenty of clover, sedge, wheat,
spelt, and the white barley which grows in wide rows. But in
5   Ithaca are no broad horselands or meadows. Goat-pasture it
is, and more lovely than horse-pasture. None of the islands
that lie out to sea is good for horse-riding or full of meadows,
least of all Ithaca.'

(b) *Odyssey ix. 19-28*

'I am Odysseus, son of Laertes, known to all men
for my cunning; my fame has gone up to heaven. My home is
Ithaca, a sunny land. In it is Mount Neriton, tree-clad, far-
seen. All around nestle many islands, very near one another –
5   Doulichion, Same, and wooded Zakynthos. Ithaca itself is
low-lying, far out in the sea towards the west; the others lie
apart, towards the rising sun. Ithaca is a rough land, but a
good nurse of real men. For myself, I cannot imagine anything
sweeter than one's own place.'

(c) *Odyssey xiii. 237-249*

'You're weak in the head, stranger, or else you've
come a long way if you ask me about *this* land. After all, it's
not off the map; many men know it, both those who live towards the sun-rise and those whose home lies the other way,
5   towards the west and the darkness. The land is rough, no
country for horse-riding; yet it's not too harsh, even though
it's not broad. There is plentiful corn here, and wine is made.

106

Always we have rainfall and plenty of dew. It's good country
for goats and oxen. There's woodland of all sorts, and water-
holes are full all the year round. And that, my friend, is why
the name of Ithaca has spread even as far as Troy, which, they
say, is distant enough from the land of Achaea.'

(d) *Odyssey xiii. 344-360*

'But come, I'll show you the rock of Ithaca, and then
you'll believe me. This place here is the haven of Phorkys, old
man of the sea, and here at the head of the creek is the long-
leaved olive-tree. And here is the wide, high-arching cave,
where you used to complete many perfect offerings to the
Nymphs. And this is Mount Neriton, forest-clad.' So she spoke,
and with divine power scattered the mist so that the land was
clear to see. Then the much-enduring Odysseus, child of the
gods, rejoiced and took pleasure in his land, and he kissed the
earth, giver of grain. At once he lifted up his hands and prayed
to the Nymphs: Nymphs of the rivers, daughters of Zeus, never
did I think to see you again; and now, my blessings on you,
with prayers of good-will. Gifts also will I give as before, if the
daughter of Zeus, Athene who provides the spoil, lets me live
and brings to manhood my son, Telemachus.'

Appreciation

1. The whole *Odyssey* is 'Ithaca-centred'. Odysseus
is driven to seek his return by a variety of reasons, including
love for his wife and son and desire for his kingdom; but behind
these lies a wanderer's picture of a 'land of lost content'. It is
interesting to observe how Homer fills in the details of this
image, not always by words or thoughts ascribed to Odysseus
himself. First there is the idea of a remote, unfertile, outer-
Hebridean type of fastness such as is described in (a), where

Telemachus, on his visit to Sparta, tells King Menelaus that Ithaca lacks the vale of Lacedaemon's rich crops. The particular, earthy words are evocative (clover, sedge, barley) and the list closes with a formulaic phrase and a metrical inversion which compels attention:

*pŭrōi' tē zéiai tĕ ĭd' ēurŭphŭĕs krĭ' lēukŏn'**

('wheat, spelt, and the white barley which grows in wide rows')

Ithaca, by contrast, is fit for goats rather than horses, and Telemachus must therefore refuse Menelaus' kingly offer of three horses and a chariot. But behind his depreciatory estimate of the qualities of his home we feel Telemachus' attachment, and it may be that the syntactical abruptness of ll.5–6 is a cover for deep feeling: 'mere goat-pasture – but more lovely than any horse-meadow'. Ithaca is less fertile even than the other islands around it, but, with an ingrained perversity which makes Menelaus smile, Telemachus loves it all the better for that. He is thus shown as having inherited his father's patriotism, and by this touch Homer makes us feel that the island's future will be in good hands.

2. Odysseus himself uses more evocative language. In (b) he is revealing his identity to the Phaeacians, who have promised to send him home in one of their magic ships, however distant that home may be. Ithaca at this moment is therefore urgently present in his imagination, and he describes his home to them in striking terms; first the tree-clad Mount Neriton which is the sailors' mark, then the small surrounding islands, which are lovingly catalogued:

Dōulĭchĭŏn tĕ Sămē tĕ kăi' hŭlēĕssă Zăkýnthŏs'

'Dulichium and Same and wooded Zakynthos'.

The vowel-sounds fall pleasantly on the ear, and we think of

---

* Cf. Passage VIII, Appreciation, 2 (note on 'spondaic ending').

Milton's similar device in *Lycidas*.*
>   Or whether thou, to our moist vows denied,
>   Sleep'st by the fable of Bellerus old,
>   Where the great vision of the guarded Mount
>   Looks toward Namancos and Bayona's hold . . .

Milton's sonorous names suggest legendary size and remoteness, while Odysseus' list rather gives affectionate detail; in his mind he is running his eye over the chart and naming places well known to him. Ithaca is low-lying, far out to the West: 'rough, but a good nurse of real men'. The tone is affectionate, and in it an important part of Odysseus' psychology is set before us.

3. It is of course quite unnecessary to spend any time on the actual geography and its problems; the question whether we are to equate Ithaca with the modern Thiaki is not of any literary importance.

4. In (c) and (d) Odysseus is in fact back in Ithaca, though he does not recognize it.** Athene, masquerading as a young Ithacan shepherd, explains the situation to him not without humour. Modern English can rarely convey both dignity and at the same time humour, although it could do so once, as in the Authorized Version of the story of Balaam's ass.*** 'The ass said unto Balaam "What have I done unto thee, that thou has smitten me these three times?" Here a sense of grievance and injured pride are both admirably conveyed, and we smile as we read. Similarly Athene in our passage pokes fun at Odysseus for not knowing his own home; and, as Stanford in his commentary says, 'There is a sly touch of humour and pathos in mentioning Troy's remoteness to this far-travelled veteran of the Trojan war.' However, it is also noticeable that, in her role as a local talking to a stranger, she praises the qualities of the island as a native would; the depreciatory tone of Telemachus' remarks in Sparta is quite

* *Lycidas*, 159-162.
** Cf. Passage XIII, Appreciation, 1.
*** *Numbers*, 22, 28.

absent. Ithaca on this occasion is said to have plentiful crops and to be well watered; in fact it is famous all over the world. The tone is that of (b).

5. Finally, in (d), the goddess disperses the cloud which has obscured Odysseus' version and shows him his home-land detail by detail. The language is warm and graphic: she mentions the harbour of Phorkys, that old man of the sea, with olive-trees looking down onto it: the cave of the Nymphs, where Odysseus used to make his offerings so long ago: and Mount Neriton, which is described in exactly the same words as Odysseus himself used in Phaeacia.

6. In these four passages the picture is taken from different angles, but the camera is moving closer all the time, until in the end we see the details of the scene through Odysseus' own eyes. The hero's long-standing desire is satisfied, and in his immediate reaction, when the local Nymphs stand foremost in his thoughts alongside Athene herself, we perceive a fundamentally good man whose dearest wish is to resume in peace the local rituals from which he has been separated so long.

7. In all four passages the language is perfectly simple and direct, and the descriptions are objective; only the adjectives show the intense force of emotion which Homer is transmitting. A particularly interesting example occurs in (d) 1.10, where Odysseus kisses the 'grain-giving' earth: the adjective is formulaic, but in this context if anywhere we may believe it to be 'positive', because Ithaca is for Odysseus more than a place: it is an idea.*

* Cf. C. P. Cavafy's poem '*Ithaca*', in *Six Poets of Modern Greece*, tr. E. Keeley and P. Sherrard (London, 1960).

Short Bibliography

Literary studies

Auerbach, E.	**Mimesis,** ch. I,* Princeton, 1953
Bassett, S. E.	**The Poetry of Homer,** Berkeley, 1938
Bowra, C. M.	**Heroic Poetry,** London, 1952
Havelock, E. A.	**Preface to Plato,** Oxford, 1963
Kirk, G. S.	**The Songs of Homer,** Cambridge, 1962. (Paperback version, **Homer and the Epic,** Cambridge, 1965)
Lord, A. B.	**Singer of Tales,** Harvard, 1960. (Paperback, New York, 1965)
Page, D. L.	**The Homeric Odyssey,** Oxford, 1955
Scholes, R. E. and Kellogg, R. L.	**The Nature of Narrative,** New York and Oxford, 1966
Stanford, W. B.	**The Ulysses Theme,** Oxford, 1963
Vries, J. P. M. L. de	**Heroic Song and Heroic Legend,** paperback, Oxford, 1959
Whitman, C. H.	**Homer and the Heroic Tradition,** Cambridge, Mass., 1958
Woodhouse, W. J.	**The Composition of Homer's Odyssey,** Oxford, 1930; reprinted, 1969

Background information

Finley, M. I.	**The World of Odysseus,** London, 1956
Wace, A. J. B. and Stubbings, F. H. (edd.)	**Companion to Homer,** London, 1963

* Reprinted in Steiner, G. and Fagles, R. (edd.), *Homer – A Collection of Critical Essays,* Englewood Cliffs, N.J., 1962 (paperback).

Critical edition of the Greek text

Stanford, W. B.   Homer: **Odyssey** i – **xii** and **xiii** – **xxiv** (2 vols),
                       London, 1947

Translations of the whole Odyssey

The following are recommended:
Fitzgerald, R.   London, 1962 (line-by-line version)
Lattimore, R.   New York and London, 1967 (line-by-line
                       version; paperback 1968)
Rieu, E. V.   Penguin Classics Series, 1946
Shaw, T. E.   Galaxy paperback, New York, 1956
(Lawrence of Arabia)

Guide to Pronunciation
and List of Greek Proper Names

Throughout the book, well-known names have been given in their traditional English form; such names are asterisked in the list which follows. Less well-known names have been transliterated from the Greek (e.g. Doulichion). There are also a few hybrids. The compromise leads to anomalies, but it seems less unpleasing than universal transliteration, which would give us Kirke for Circe and Kuklops instead of the familiar Cyclops.

There are consequent problems over pronunciation, and in what follows both an English and an approximate Greek pronunciation have been indicated. In some cases however a mixture of both pronunciations has become traditional.

Vowels

Ancient Greek vowel-sounds were more like those of modern Italian than their English equivalents, but our own vowels usually provide a tolerable substitute if we remember the following points:

1) The distinction between long and short vowels (cf. Intro. 6) is fundamental.

2) In Greek, a is always short (as in 'fat') or long (as in 'fàther'). The English a as in 'mate' is not heard.

3) Greek e is always short (as in 'pet') or long (sound as in 'tray'). The English e as in 'theme' is not heard.

4) In Anglicized names, i and y should both be pronounced, if short, as in 'thick'; if long, sound as in 'pie'. In Greek, the short i is as in 'thick', and the long i is sounded as in 'sweet'.

5) All Greek vowels should be pronounced separately (e.g. Ămphíthĕē) unless they are marked as diphthongs (e.g. Âeâeă).

Diphthongs

Pairs of vowels pronounced as one are marked by the sign ⌢
Pronounce as follows:

ae: (not found in Greek); in English, sound as ee
ai: in Greek, sound as in English 'hire'.
au: in Greek, sound as in English 'bough'.
    in English, sound as in English 'lawn'.
ei: in Greek, sound as in English 'they'.
eu: in both languages, sound as in English 'dew'.
oe: (not found in Greek); in English, sound as ee.
oi: in Greek, sound as in English 'boy'.
ou: in Greek, sound as in English 'moon'.

Consonants

Greek consonants were pronounced more or less like their
English equivalents, with the following exceptions:

c, g: always hard. (In Anglicized names they are sometimes
    softened, and this is indicated where necessary.)
ch: as in Scottish 'loch'. (English readers usually mispro-
    nounce as k.)
th: pronounced softly, as in 'thin'.
s: always soft (not as z).
x: pronounce as ks, not gz.
z: pronounced as sd, though English readers often give ds or
    dz.

Note that, as in Italian, double consonants must both be
sounded.

List of Greek Proper Names

* Ăchíllēs
* Ǣeáèă
* Ǣeŏlus
* Ālcínŏus (soft 'c' in English)
  Āmphíthēē
* Andrŏmăchē̆ (final 'e' long in Greek, short in English)
  Antíphătēs
* Ăpŏ́llō
  Árgŏs
  Ārtắkĭē
* Ártĕmĭs
  Árȳbās
* Ăthénĕ̆ (final 'e' long in Greek, short in English)
* Âutŏ́lȳcus
  Bŏmbúkā
* Cắlȳpsō
* Chărȳ́bdĭs
* Círcĕ̆ (soft 'c's in English. Final 'e' long in Greek, short in English).
* Cnóssus (modern English sometimes gives short 'o')
* Cȳ́clops (soft initial 'c' in English)
* Cȳ́zĭcus (soft initial 'c' in English)
* Dēmŏ́dŏcus
  Dŏ́lōn
  Dōulíchĭŏn
  Ēlpénōr
  Ĕrĕ́cthe͡us
* Ĕrȳmánthus
* Ēumắe͡us
* Ēurȳclê͡ıa
* Górtyn̦
* Hēpha͡ĕstus
* Hérmēs
  Īkắrĭŏs
  Īlĭŏne͡ûs
  Īnō
  Írŏs
* Íthăcă

115

Kíkŏnĕs
Krŏ́nŏs
Ktésĭŏs
* Lăcĕdǽmon (soft 'c' in English)
* Lăértes
* Laéstrȳgóníă (Greek, Laìstrūgóníā)
Lắmŏs
Létō
Mắlĕā or Mălḗiă
* Mắrăthon
Mḗdōn
* Mĕnĕláus
* Mínōs
* Mȳcénáè (soft 'c' in English)
* Naûsĭcăā
Nérĭtŏn
* Ŏdȳ́ssêus
* Ōgȳ́gĭa (second 'g' is soft in English)
Órmĕnŏs
* Ōrtȳ́gĭa (soft 'g' in English)
* Parnássus
* Penḗlŏpĕ̆ (final 'e' long in Greek, short in English)
* Phăèácia (soft 'c' in English)
* Phémĭus
Phĭlŏètĭŏs
* Phŏènícia (soft 'c' in English)
Phórkȳs
* Príam
* Pȳ́los
Sắmē
* Scămánder
* Schḗrĭa
* Scȳ́lla ('sc' pronounced as 's' in English)
* Sídon
* Sírens
* Spárta
Sȳ́rĭē
* Tắphĭans
* Tăȳ́gĕtus (soft 'g' in English)
* Tēlĕ̆măchus
Thĭákī
* Zăkȳ́nthus
* Zeûs

Index of Literary Topics discussed in the Introduction and Appreciations

The first part of each entry refers to the Introduction or Passage in question, the second to the paragraph numbers, which run continuously throughout each Appreciation.

Index

Minoan/Mycenaean reminiscence:
see Depth of narrative
Monosyllables: III.1; IX.2; XI.7
Moods: see Colour of narrative
Moralizing, implicit: XIX.2
Musical accompaniment: Intro. 8
Names, invented: X.2
Narrative, immediacy of: XVI.3;
XVII.2, 5
—technique: XI. 1—5;
XIII.2; XVI.7;
XVII.1—6
Neutrality of diction: see Diction
Objectivity: see Realism
Oblique view: see Description
Onomatopeia: I.1; II.5 f.n.; III.1;
IV.3; VIII.2; IX.2, 7; XI.6, 14;
XII.3; XX.2
Oral techniques: Intro. 2, 3 cf. Bards
Originality in Homer: Intro.10, 14;
XVII.8; XIX.3
Over-run lines: see Enjamb-
ment, s.v. Metrical
techniques
Paradise-theme: see Land of
plenty, s.v. Themes
'Particularizing' details: see
Details
Pathos: XI.2; XV.4
Periphrases: see Kennings
Personification: IV.1; XI.2;
XVI.2 cf. Deities,
anthropomorphic
Pictorial detail: I.3; II.2—4;
IV.2—3; V.1; VII.3; XI.2;
XVII.2—7; XVIII.5; XIX.4
Plot: Intro. 3; III.5
'Posturing': Intro. 3; XI.1
Psychological analysis: IV.1;
XVI.2; XVII.2 cf.
Characterization
Quantities: see Metrical
techniques

Rapport (Odysseus/Telemachus):
XVII.9; XIX.1
Realism: III.2; IV.2; IX.2;
XV.2; XVII.7; XIX.1, 2
Reality and unreality: VIII.4, 5
'Recession' of narratives: XVII.5
Reminiscence, deliberate: XI.12, 14;
XIII.2
Repetitions: see Comparisons,
Retention
Restraint: see Feeling
Retention (double version etc.):
III.4; V.3; VI.2, 4; VIII.1;
IX.5; XI.2, 5; XIV. 1—3;
XVII.2 cf. Contradictions,
Doublets, Themes
Reticence: Intro. 16; XVI.7;
XIX.2
'Revivified' epithets: see Epithets
Rhetoric: XII.8; XVI.7
Ring-composition: XVII.3—4
River-theme: see Themes
Scansion: see Metrical
techniques
Sententiousness: IX.6; XV.8
Sentimentality: XV.1
Similes—general: V.4; VI.1, 5;
VII.3; XI.2; XII.4;
XVIII.3; XIX.1
—daily life as basis: V.4;
IX.4; XI.4, 9; XIX.4
—'inverted': IV.2
—'long-tailed': XI.3;
XVII.4 f.n.
—novel application: XIII.4
—'slow-starting': XI.3
—superlative by means of:
VI.1; XVI.4
—unparalleled: III.1
Stock epithets: see Epithets
Stock passages: Intro. 3; I.2, 5;
V.2; VII.4 cf. Epithets,
Formulae

119